WALTER C. KAISER, JR.

Have You Seen the Power of God Lately?

Lessons for Today from Elijah

Here's Life Publishers

Published by
HERE'S LIFE PUBLISHERS, INC.
P.O. Box 1576
San Bernardino, CA 92402

HLP Product No. 951608
©1987, Walter C. Kaiser
All Rights reserved.
Printed in the United States of America

Library of Congress Cataloging-in-Publication Data
Kaiser, Walter C.
     Have you seen the power of God lately?

     Includes indexes.
     1. Elijah (Biblical prophet)   I. Title.
BS580.E4K35 1987   222'.50924   86-22745
ISBN 0-89840-167-4 (pbk.)

FOR MORE INFORMATION, WRITE:

L.I.F.E. — P.O. Box A399, Sydney South 2000, Australia
Campus Crusade for Christ of Canada — Box 300, Vancouver, B.C., V6C 2X3, Canada
Campus Crusade for Christ — Pearl Assurance House, 4 Temple Row, Birmingham, B2 5HG, England
Lay Institute for Evangelism — P.O. Box 8786, Auckland 3, New Zealand
Great Commission Movement of Nigeria — P.O. Box 500, Jos, Plateau State Nigeria, West Africa
Campus Crusade for Christ International — Arrowhead Springs, San Bernardino, CA 92414, U.S.A.

Have You Seen the Power of God Lately?

TO
MRS. LOIS ARMSTRONG

For extraordinary service to our Lord
as my administrative assistant for seven years now
and a total of twenty years' service to the seminary.

"Give her the reward she has earned,
and let her works bring her praise
[in the pulpits and mission stations of the earth]."

Proverbs 31:31 (NIV)

Contents

Before We Begin . . .

"Where now is the Lord, the God of Elijah?" asked Elisha, as he set out to fill the recently vacated post of his master.

And we too must ask the same question of our generation once again, for the same mighty power of God that had operated in the days of Elijah is now available for believers on the same basis it was offered to him.

Unfortunately, all too little of that power and dynamism is being evidenced in Christianity today. This situation is the need we hope to address with these eleven studies in the life of Elijah from 1 Kings 17 through 2 Kings 2, with special attention also being given to the Elijah prophecies in Malachi 4, Luke 9 and Revelation 11.

It is my sincere desire that these studies will be used in elective Sunday school classes, home Bible studies, private devotions, and pastors' preparations for expository messages on this wonderful section of the Scriptures. For too long now the church and the laity at large have cheated themselves out of the fabulous riches that are stored in the Old Testament for guidance of those who need to compete in the modern world.

These truths are so plain, practical, and positive that they will astonish most who have not recently looked to the Old Testament for a challenge and direction for their lives. I urge you to study these chapters with your Bible open. If these studies prove to be as helpful to you as I have found them to be in my own life, share what you've learned with another person or group. Only in this manner will the current famine for the Word of God cease.

Be sure to read through the biblical text several times. Ask yourself two key questions to begin: (1) "Can I write down the purpose or goal of this section of 1 Kings and how it fits in with the purpose of the whole book?" (2) "Am I able to identify the smaller units of thought within the Elijah section of this first book of Kings?" Usually these units correspond to chapter divisions or episodes within those chapters, but this is not always so. Then you should be able to divide off the paragraphs in each of these units while noting the key idea in each of the paragraphs.

Should you wish to know anything about the background on any of the places, persons or times mentioned in 1 Kings 17 to 2 Kings 2, you should consult a Bible atlas, Bible dictionary or Bible encyclopedia. Often these resource materials can be of some help, but do not let any of these secondary tools overpower you and drown out the voice of our Lord from the Holy Scriptures themselves.

Remember, God has promised to bless His Word, but this does not mean that the same blessing will automatically carry over into all of our secondary resources. The story is told of a woman of plain-but-devout lifestyle who once borrowed a commentary from her pastor and then returned it with thanks and the observation that it was amazing how much light the Bible shed on the *commentary!*

I exaggerate this point to emphasize how much more important is the inductive study of the Bible itself. There is much that can be gleaned from other sources when they are used in an appropriate way. But let us never let them distract from our straightforward study of the Bible itself.

My prayer is that the Lord may shine through the passages of Scripture again and that we may behold the magnificence of His power and His presence in our midst. A whole new view of the greatness of God would be more than adequate to revive Christ's people and to set us afire once again with a revived sense of mission and purpose.

It remains only to tell the reader that unless otherwise noted, all translations of the Scriptures are my own. I also wish to thank Leslie H. Stobbe for his encouragement over the years and the part he has played in bringing this manuscript to the light of day.

1

Whose Word Can You Trust These Days?
1 Kings 17:1-7

There is a great line in one of Charles Schulz's *Peanuts* cartoons. It is raining "cats and dogs" outside the window when Lucy asks the most profound question of the day: "Boy, look at it rain. What if it floods the whole world?" Fully up to the occasion as usual, Linus, the resident theologian, answers that a worldwide flood is impossible since Genesis nine promises that God will never again flood the earth. Obviously relieved, Lucy sighs, "You've taken a great load off my mind . . ." Linus's final summation: "Sound theology has a way of doing that!"

And that is just what the issue is all about: Whose word can you trust these days? What makes one word more dependable than another word, for that is all you hear — words, words, words! They all sound so common and so familiar that eventually they all become one big blur, especially since so many of the words turn out, on examination, to be so undependable and just plain wrong.

How many times have you been promised one thing or another by a merchant or a car repair shop only to find that their words were not worth a single moment of trust? It is time we asked, "Whose word can you trust these days?"

But that is the focus of the first episode recorded in the life of Elijah. Like a bolt out of the blue, 1 Kings 17:1 suddenly surprises us with a new turn in the narrative of this book. There, all of a sudden, is a man whom we have never met before, a man merely described as a Tishbite from the inhabitants of Gilead. Even the name Tishbite sounds more like some kind of crackers than any territory we are familiar with. And what little we know about Gilead does not help either, since that area east of the Sea of Galilee is strictly out of the way and not where the real movers and shakers lived and wielded their influence. Regardless, here he comes, ready or not. So the text begins: "Now Elijah the Tishbite, from the inhabitants of Gilead, said to Ahab. . . ."

"Said to Ahab"? Ahab was the king. What was this country bumpkin doing in the palace? And who said he could address the king? Elijah told Ahab, ". . . neither dew nor rain in the next years except by my word." What kind of talk was that for some untutored, uncultured Tishbite to be directing at the king of Israel? Why should Elijah's word be trusted any more than anyone else's word? But that is just the point.

THE WORD OF THE LORD IS DEPENDABLE

1 Kings 17 was not preserved to give us a quaint story about olden times. Rather, it was narrated so that both the people in the writer's day and we in ours might come to appreciate in a new way what this text repeats four times in each of its four episodes: "The word of the LORD . . . is dependable" (verses 2,8,16,24).

Actually, there are five separate scenes in 1 Kings 17:

1. In the palace (verse 1)
2. By the brook Cherith (verses 2-7)
3. At the town gate of Zarephath, Phoenicia (verses 8-13)
4. In the widow's home day after day (verses 14-15)
5. In the midst of tragedy at the widow's home (verses 16-24)

What binds all five scenes together is not the character

and actions of the recluse Elijah; instead, it is the presence and power of the word of God. Moreover, the key line in the whole narrative is saved for the last scene, and what the prophetic writer of Holy Scripture wanted to emphasize is placed in the concluding speech of the deeply grateful widow. Said she: "Now I know that you are a man of God, and that the word of the LORD in your mouth is the truth" (verse 24).

Each episode deserves its own analysis since each makes a different point about the dependability of the word of God. The first begins in what is probably the audience-hall of the king of Israel. There we picture our rustic Tishbite making a very unceremonious entrance with a most abbreviated and tortuously truncated message for the king: "No dew and no rain."

Now we moderns have had to put up with a lot from our hard-working, but often-befuddled, weathermen; but who is this one called Elijah? Who asked him to predict the weather? No dew or rain for *years?* That has to be one of the worst weather forecasts on record. Nevertheless, that is what he said.

This man Elijah was even more audacious; while standing in the presence of royalty, he had the nerve to speak of an awareness of a royalty that exceeded that of King Ahab! Surely that is the quickest way to get tossed out on one's ear, much less to be taken seriously. But that is what Elijah did.

He began: "As the LORD, the God of Israel lives, in whose presence I stand . . ." In so stating, this rustic made three claims:

1. The God he served was a living Lord.
2. This Lord had a special relationship to Israel, for He was the "God of Israel."
3. The man from Gilead was more conscious of being in God's presence than he was of all the pageantry, pomp and circumstance of Ahab's royal palace where this message was being delivered.

Thus it happened that while the nation was going crazy after Baal and the gods of the Canaanites instead of following the living Lord, one man dared to raise his voice in strong protest on behalf of the one who had sent him. In fact, the very name of Elijah symbolized his mission; it meant "Yahweh (*i.e.,* Jehovah) is my God." Whether his parents had named him Elijah as an act of faith or under prophetic impulse, we cannot tell. But his name certainly stood as a stake for godliness and truth when the times stood for everything else.

THE PRICE OF DISOBEDIENCE

How then, you ask, did that word of God vindicate itself during these times and especially in such a short vignette as this opening verse appears to be?

The answer is provided by the Scriptures which were already a part of the community's heritage. Indeed, Moses had warned years prior to this episode that "The LORD will strike you with . . . drought. . . . The sky over you will be bronze, the ground beneath you iron. The LORD will turn the rain of your country into dust and powder; it will come down from the skies until you are ruined" (Deuteronomy 28:22-24). All of this would happen if Israel did not obey the Lord and carry out the implications of their covenantal relationship.

In order to capture the attention of hearts that had become oblivious to the gracious hand of their omnipotent provider, the Lord removed some of the assumed gifts of life from them, for only God can give or withhold the dew and rain. But there is more here than meets the eye at first. There is also a theology of the soil that goes all the way back to the Garden of Eden.

There, God made man out of the dust of the ground. But when man fell in his sin, a strange thing happened: His sin affected the dirt just as much as he was affected! The curse that fell on mankind also fell on the soil and on nature itself. No wonder, then, that Paul describes all of creation in agony and deep birth pangs, groaning in travail, anxiously waiting and hoping for the final redemption of man at the second coming of our Lord Jesus Christ (Romans 8:19-22).

Therefore, when men and women hurt, even nature itself goes into convulsions just as it did at the fall. Nature becomes one of God's indicators that something is out of whack and needs immediate spiritual attention; if men and women do not get right with God, neither can harmony be restored or substantial healing come to the created order itself.

Whose word can we trust? We can trust the word of the Lord. His word is dependable in the judgments and threats that He pronounces. Thus, when we desert our God we may fully expect that He will carry out his judgments even as He announced them in the Old Testament. For even though the theocracy in Israel no longer exists, the whole world is still the sphere in which Yahweh demonstrates that He is still the King over all even though its fullest manifestation awaits the second coming of our Lord.

The way that word came into effect was through the prayers of one man, Elijah, whom James describes as a regular man with the same kind of real problems and weaknesses as ours (James 5:17). The point is, however, that Elijah prayed earnestly. In response to this divinely implanted desire to pray in this manner, God withheld rain for three-and-a-half years!

Since Elijah is a man just like us, James urges us not only to pray in a similar manner, but also to put heavy stock in every word God has spoken. It would be sheer nonsense and a crime of first rank if we who know the Lord would turn around and in life or action act as if His words were just like anyone else's words. Cynically placing God's words in the same class as the barrage of lies and half-truths we hear all too frequently today will make us vulnerable to the same judgments announced by Elijah. God's word is surely dependable — yes, even when we desert and abandon our God.

GOD REMOVES HIS MESSENGER

The throne scene ends without recording Ahab's response, but we don't need to have that recorded. Ahab's actions are only too clear for us to be delayed by speeches bordering on the trivial. But that was not the end of the majestic and magnificent word of God. Verse 2 begins with a new inbreaking of the word as Elijah is directed to leave and hide in the ravine of Cherith.

Why would God direct His messenger to leave the public scene and to hide? Was He worried about protecting His messenger? In fact, why didn't He send Elijah on a whole new offensive, complete with mass meetings and all that goes with it? What would seclusion from the public eye accomplish?

Surprisingly, Elijah was not told to hide in order to grant him protection from a wrathful Ahab or from vindictive interlopers. Rather, God hid him to prevent people from hearing the word of God which they had come to despise — or at least to disregard — which amounts to the same thing.

If Israel did not wish to act on the basis of that word,

then God did not wish them to be falsely comforted with the repeated hearing of that word as if hearing, in itself, could in some liturgical or magical way sanctify and condone all the evil the people were embracing. Thus God sometimes removes from the public eye and ear those who faithfully minister His word to speed up the alarm among those who are not altogether tone-deaf to that word of God.

Just as it was in the days of young Samuel when "the word of God was rare" (1 Samuel 3:1), so it happened in Elijah's day. Some gripe so about those who minister God's word so faithfully. They wish that these ministers would be quiet and would never "harp on" the unpleasant aspects of Scripture. Whenever this opinion begins to form the sentiment of the majority, especially among the household of faith, we can be sure that the indictment of Amos 8:11-12 is not far off for that culture, people, or times: "The days are coming, declares the LORD of Hosts, when I will send a famine through the land — not a famine of food or a thirst for water, but a famine of hearing the words of the LORD."

There is a brighter prospect, however, for those who will repent and turn back to the Lord. That reversal of conditions was noted by the prophet Isaiah: "Although the LORD gives you the bread of adversity and the waters of affliction, your teachers will be hidden no more; with your own eyes you will see them" (Isaiah 30:20).

So the word of the Lord is still dependable even when we do not deserve God's ministers. Accordingly, God often directs His servants to leave the public scene and thus the word of God becomes extremely rare and difficult to find. So it was that the prophet who appeared almost out of thin air disappeared into thin air and the king was relieved of any further words of judgment. Or so it seemed for the moment.

PRESERVING THE PROPHET

Elijah was no deserter or shirker of his duty: he was commanded by God to leave the area. Thus, even without the usual prophetic formula ("Then the word of the LORD came to [Elijah]"), it is still clear that we are dealing with a prophet of God. And therein also lies the marvelous point of grace found in this story. It is the *office* of prophet that is being maintained, and that is good news for all who fear that this text speaks only of judgment. When God preserves His prophet, He preserves him for another day when the word can again be freely given and joyfully received. The *office* is maintained for the benefit of the people.

Elijah, then, was no privileged character or a special "pet" of God; Israel (and eventually all of us) also could receive the "special treatment" (God's grace) which many people mistakenly believe can be experienced only by a mighty, chosen prophet.

But why did God send Elijah to the ravine and brook Cherith? God had made plans to provide for His prophet. There would be water from the brook Cherith. There would be heavenly waiters (well, there would be those birds that would bring food every morning and evening).

Birds? Ravens?

Didn't God remember His own teaching that ravens were an abomination?[1] Why couldn't God have used people to smuggle in food, or, if nothing else worked, send angels? But birds? Surely Elijah would now say, "This job is for the birds!"

But there is no such claptrap by God's servant. Instead, we see Elijah's faithful obedience and ready acceptance of all God's provisions. Some have taken more affront at the ravens than Elijah did. These modern scholars have tried to reduce their own embarrassment over the fact that God would use ravens by noting that the Hebrew word for ravens *(oreb)* could be read as Orebites or Arabians. But there are no grounds for suggesting this variant reading and the ravens will have to stand in spite of these rationalistic vultures.

What was God's point in using ravens? Surely they were no mere ploys in the plot. Perhaps they were used to show Elijah, and us, that God is Lord over all creation. The same Lord who could shut off the rain was likewise in control of even His winged creatures, and they could be commanded to serve those made in the image of God. The same generation that worried so much about appeasing a local god Baal (allegedly the god of rain, dew and fertility) needed to learn once again that only God gives life and breath to all. But more than this, the prophet himself was also being prepared for his one great day of contest with the false prophets of Baal. The same Lord who could command birds to feed Elijah was the identical one in control of fire and rain in heaven. He is the Lord of all creation.

We must be on our guard, as M. B. Van't Veer warns us, against the sin of generalization:

> It is all too easy to enlarge the circle the Lord has drawn around His servant Elijah, who was an instrument of *special* revelation, to include everyone who struggles with difficulties in this life. We then comfort ourselves by assuming that we will be protected just as Elijah was protected. We have no such guarantee. In fact, we are too hasty here in our eagerness for comfort. We comfort each other by saying that the Lord will provide for His children in such a way that not one of them will ever die of hunger because they will always be supplied with bread and water. At the right time the Lord will open his hand so everyone will eat and be filled.[2]

Such a generalization moves beyond legitimate application or universalizing of the text, for it fails to note the unique circumstances of the *office* and the *mission* given to Elijah. It also takes what is miraculous and turns it into a normative experience which all can count on continually. One need only recall what had already happened to the prophets of the Lord as a result of Jezebel's fury. But worst of all, it fails to listen carefully to the purpose of the narrative, for God did not designate that this episode be inscripturated in order to comfort those who are hungry and thirsty worldwide and in all times.

PRESERVING THE WORD

Instead, this narrative is meant to teach us just the reverse: "[Men and women] do not live by bread alone, but by every word that proceeds from the mouth of the LORD" (Deuteronomy 8:3). In preserving Elijah, God was graciously preserving His word for another day when it could be received more joyfully by the same audience that saw little or no relevance to its publication previously.

Tragedy, alas, also struck the prophet, for the brook Cherith dried up as well. Even an Elijah could not demand the mercies of God; these mercies were lent, not deserved, by the prophet or us.

Why did the brook dry up if God had taken so much trouble to keep His message alive this long? Would that effort all be wasted now? No, God had further plans, but in the meantime the prophet must have also felt some of the calamities that he had announced. Only then could he feel what the people felt and be part of their calamities. When God allows His messengers to experience the same trials as His offenders, the difference is only in the *use* made of these experiences. For the offenders the trial was to lead to repentance; for the prophet the trial was to lead to a deeper consciousness of the grace and power of God while the reality of sharing the people's misery proved his real identification with them.

What rings clearly through this section (verses 1-7) is that the word of God is still dependable — yes, even when we don't deserve God's messengers. For while the Lord may test His servants with some of the same extremities that occasioned the message, He will effectively keep alive the message that is to be announced again in the future. For the nation of Israel in Elijah's day, that word would be scarce only temporarily.

WHOSE WORD CAN YOU TRUST?

1 Kings 17:1-7

1. To what extent do you think the sin of a nation today affects the fortunes of nature, the prosperity and safety of the nation, and the citizens of the nation? Can you cite evidence of such effects in our modern culture?

2. In what ways has the word of the Lord proven dependable in your life? Can you think of a warning from the Bible that came true because of a scriptural principle you violated? A promise from the Bible that God fulfilled?

3. What are some of the ways believers tend to demean and belittle the reliability of the word of God in our day — even in the church?

4. How will a right view of the warnings and promises of God affect your personal prayer life? Your social conscience? Your work and home? Your sharing Christ with others?

2

The Widow and The Word
1 Kings 17:8-24

Have you ever found yourself wondering if God's promises were meant only for spiritual giants such as Elijah?

If you've ever questioned whether God's word is just as reliable for the "little guy," then you'll be especially interested in this next episode in Elijah's life.

It is startling that God made no use of Jewish believers during the whole time Elijah was at the brook even though we learn that there were 7000 who had not bowed the knee to Baal. We are all the more shocked to read that God directed His servant to go into gentile territory — to Zarephath, a suburb of Sidon in ancient Phoenicia, modern Lebanon.

The irony of this proposal is that Sidon was the very hometown from which Ahab's scheming queen, Jezebel, had come. In fact, her father, Ethbaal, was king in that city and territory (1 Kings 16:31). No wonder Matthew Henry has such glee saying, "To show Jezebel the impotency of her malice, God will find a hiding place for His servant in her country."

But there is more here. Zarephath must have a meaning of its own, for Elijah was specifically sent there by God, passing up all the widows in Israel (Luke 4:25-26). Moreover, God "commanded" a widow woman who had next to nothing to provide him with food. Surely, here we have another hint in the Old Testament that God's plan of salvation is meant for the gentiles. Not only did God lead Elijah to gentile territory, but He also led him to a *woman,* and a widow at that.

This woman was preparing her last meal for herself and her son when the prophet accosted her in the city gate. Thus once again, if there was to be any help here, it would not depend on the natural resources of the woman. Everything would depend solely on God's commanding and electing word. Just as God had commanded the ravens, so He now commanded the widow. The word of God is not dependent on us or on those around us; we are totally dependent on it.

GIVING FROM POVERTY

We are not told how the prophet recognized who the person was that he was being sent to. Was she distinguishable by the type of clothes she was wearing or by the state of her poverty? It doesn't really matter. What does matter is that the very small request made of her by the prophet at their first encounter turned out to be an all-embracing demand. Indeed, everything this woman had would now be requisitioned in the service of the living God.

At first there was the mere request for a little water in a jar. Have you ever noticed how God helps us face up to more challenging demands by grading His requests of us? Simpler and easier tasks are assigned before the more difficult ones so that faith's encouragement might work for those later, harder tasks.

Of course, even here in Zarephath water was in short supply, for the drought was felt in all the countries surrounding Israel as well. The sin of God's people rarely affects just believers; the godless also suffer and so it happened in this case. The life of the believing community is never entirely unrelated to the "world." Nor are the fortunes of nations entirely independent of the existence of the believing body of Christ. When judgment must be meted out to a backslidden church, then mark it well that the protecting shadow over the nations may also be removed as well and the time of "common grace" may well be past and the time of judgment begun.

The widow did not pause to indulge in politics. She could easily have rejoined, "How is it that you, being a Jew, would ask of me, a Phoenician, a drink?" On the contrary, she dropped her sorrowful task of gathering a few sticks so that she and her son could eat their last meal and went immediately to aid this stranger — this Jew! It would be no more different from an Israeli asking a Lebanese for a drink today. This in itself must indicate that already, prior to the arrival of Elijah, God had started to work on the heart of this gentile woman in the first movements of faith.

Thus God will now provide by the power of His word from such unexpected places, unexpected persons, and in such unexpected ways. And the woman who responded with such alacrity is now given an added request. The prophet called after her, "Would you also bring me a cookie?" Well, not quite. But the request for some bread did bring up the most grievous question in the woman's life.

She answered, "As surely as the LORD (note the use of the covenant name for God which was usually reserved to indicate a personal relationship to the Lord) your God lives, I don't have any bread — only a handful of flour in a jar and a little oil in a jug. I am gathering a few sticks to take home and make a meal for myself and my son, that we may eat it — and die" (verse 12).

Very rarely has our situation been as desperate as this woman's, yet we too must learn what she would realize about the dependability of the word of God. It is clear that she knew she was speaking with a Jew, for she said, "the Lord *your* God." Neither did Elijah try to soft-peddle this possible barrier, for he responded in verse 14, "This is what the LORD, the God of Israel says." This Phoenician gentile had to learn what the Samaritan woman learned in John 4:22: "Salvation is from the Jews." This is not to say that the Jews were God's special "pets" or that He had favorites; they were the vehicles of the gracious word that was to be for all the nations (Genesis 12:3). Indeed, theirs was an election, but an election for *service*.

GOD'S WORD: ALL THE PROOF WE NEED

God's word of promise to this woman in this situation

was that the flour would not be exhausted and the oil would not run dry until it began to rain once again. The guarantee for this special announcement was the word of the God of Israel. And, marvel of marvels, the woman asked for no other proof, but went and did as she was commanded by the word of God (verse 15). When asked to give everything, this woman and son, who were at death's door, gave all. Nevertheless, the demand of God was accompanied by a promise. The law of the kingdom is: "To him who has will more be given" (Matthew 13:12).

We are still struck by the fact that God "commanded" this widow to supply His servant with food. She also used that special name for God: LORD, or Yahweh. Even though she said "your" God, we must not put too much stock in that word as if it implied distance between her and the God of Israel, for the same formula is used by righteous Obadiah in Elijah's presence (1 Kings 18:10). The whole matter is very intriguing even if we cannot finally pronounce on whether she was a believer based on these few words. But this much is clear: She had moved far enough in her own search for God to be specially singled out and favored by Yahweh to receive further confirmation that the word of God was altogether true and thoroughly dependable. Thus this section ends just as it began with the word of God in control. The flour and the oil did not run dry, observes verse 16, "in keeping with the word of the LORD spoken by Elijah."

Note that oil here is not the emblem of the Holy Spirit, for this would be to diminish the purpose for which God had had this section entered into our Scriptures. Oil is now the indication of the powerful presence of the miracle-working word of God, for just as the same Lord multiplied the five barley loaves and two small fish in another day (Matthew 14:19,20), He just as effectively demonstrated the power of His word in this situation. Indeed, as Isaiah would promise on a later day, "My word shall not return empty, but it shall accomplish that for which it was sent" (Isaiah 55:11).

Thus we have seen that the word of God is true and dependable in its judgments, in its commands, and in its promises. But we must see it one more time and in one more episode in this text: It can look ugly death right in the eye and triumph over it.

A TOUGHER TEST

The transitional word in verse 17 is all but smothered in some of our translations. "It was after these things" that the widow's son took sick — so sick that he stopped breathing. That is serious; indeed, fatal. What then is the connection between these two sections? Must we conclude, as some Christians or despisers of Christianity do, that we must pay a price for our joys, blessings and miracles? If things are going well now, just wait until the other shoe drops?

Horrors! How could we have such a low view of God? Rather, the text specifically refers to "these things" in order to show us how gently God prepares us for the next, often harder step of faith.

The unmistakable evidence of the love of God in the flour and oil test became the grounds for trust in that dependable word of God in this next test. The widow knew that Elijah had spoken the word of God just like we often know that the word of God has been spoken in our hearing. But we, like this widow, fail to recall the power of that word in the midst of the next trial and therefore we must be taught the same lesson all over again and in a more dramatic way.

Interestingly enough, while the word of God had suffered a setback and had for all intents and purposes come to a standstill in Israel, it was now blazing forth in all its power in a heathen, gentile territory. It was as if that word leaped over the traditional hurdles and suddenly established itself on the soil and in the hearts of those who would have appeared to be, by any contemporary standards of theology of that day, a non-kosher work. But God's word knows no such boundaries. The word had specifically focused on all the world when it had first been given as a promise to Abraham (Genesis 12:3).

But the death of the boy did introduce more than a mere riddle into the life of this widow who had been so kind. Even the prophet appeared to be taken back a bit in verse 20 when he remonstrated for a brief moment with God, asking why this new tragedy had been visited on the woman. It would have been all too easy for the prophet to have lashed out in pent-up frustration at the widow: "Woman, I didn't do anything to your son. Why are you blaming me for his death? Don't you realize that I could be standing before kings right now? And what do

I get instead? The tight quarters of this small house. Talk about cabin fever! I'm sick and tired of just sitting around when I could be active in some kind of work. Now I have you coming down on my head with all of your questions and accusations."

But there was none of this from Elijah. To the anxious queries and words of self-accusation he kindly retorted: "Give me your son."

What would he do now? Had he ever been faced before with a corpse? But this was no time for philosophical or theological discussion. The word of God had too firm a grip on the prophet to allow him to seek any other path than to appeal to that same source in this deep moment of need. This man who is "a man of similar nature with ourselves" (James 5:17) seized the word of promise and prayed, "O Lord God, let this child's life come into him again."

A MIRACLE AFFIRMS GOD'S PROMISE

If the widow had not realized it before, she certainly could see now that this miracle was being performed so that she might come to trust the God who now made Himself known even to gentiles. God is indeed wise in what He allows. He is also mighty in what He does.

The promise of God had been to give life, for the flour and oil would not run dry until it began to rain again. It was this promise that the prophet seized with both hands as he cried to God in prayer. If God and His word were to be vindicated, this widow must see life, not death. It is no wonder that the prophet felt the strength of the riddle that faced her and himself. The one reality and the one fact which must triumph over every other event these two main characters faced was the reality that the word of God was reliable and true in everything it affirmed.

Elijah's prayer became the occasion, but not the reason, for restoring the widow's son back to life. It is true that Jesus taught, "Whatever you ask in prayer, you will receive, if you have faith" (Matthew 21:22). But faith here, and for Elijah, was not faith in faith — a pulling of oneself up by the bootstraps. Biblical faith was and is always a matter of being grounded in Scripture, the Word of God. The promises of Scripture were not meant to excuse us from prayer or to let us know what it was in the kingdom of God that we could take for granted.

Instead, they were given so that we might be taught what it is that we ought to pray for and what it is our faith could cling to.

The believer can ask anything — provided it is based on the Word of God. All other prayers are prayed uselessly or selfishly and cannot claim these same guarantees. Elijah pleaded: (1) a special relationship with God ("my God"); (2) the mercies and compassion of the same Lord who had sent him; and (3) that the will of God would allow this boy's life to return to him. And the text succinctly observes: "The LORD heard Elijah's cry and the boy's life returned to him and he lived" (verse 22). This is because "The eyes of the Lord are on the righteous and his ears are attentive to their prayer" (1 Peter 3:12), and also because "This is the assurance we have in approaching God: that if we ask anything according to his will, he hears us. And if we know that he hears us — whatever we ask — we know that we have what we asked of him" (1 John 5:14,15).

Neither should we count the act of bodily contact as some significant feature of the record that perhaps tips us off to the presence of some magic or hidden power. The reason for his action is difficult to explain, but the Bible merely reports that he did this without making it a normative feature or without urging us to use some similar technique when we are in a similar situation. It was the Lord who brought the child back again and not the technique of any man.

THE WIDOW'S CONCLUSION

No longer can we be in any doubt as to what 1 Kings 17 is all about. The writer has left the climactic statement for the final moment in the chapter. The widow exclaims upon seeing her son restored back from the clutches of death: "Now I know that you are a man of God and that the word of the LORD from your mouth is the truth" (verse 24). Thus she acknowledges the *office* of the prophet (he was "a man of God") and the absolute *reliability* of that word.

Strange, indeed, that while the nation best prepared to receive the truth expressed by this grateful widow was far away from acknowledging anything close to it, God had raised up someone to praise His name and witness the dependability of His word from those who were "not a people." God continues to do so in every generation. We should never fear that the cause of Christ will go begging or that it will despair for lack of someone to carry that word. God can and will raise up from the stones, if He must, those who will trust Him. His cause is not tied down to the fortunes of America, evangelicalism, fundamentalism, or the Christian church in the West. He will triumph; the only question on which there is any doubt is whether we will be faithful and will thereby participate with Him in that triumph.

2 Kings 2:14 asks: "Where is the LORD God of Elijah?" Is He not the same God? And is not His word just as dependable today as it ever was? If we in our generation wish to rise to the challenge of this magnificent moment in history, we must not fail to treat that word of God as more than food itself. We must not act in any way that betrays that we are somewhat dubious about the dependability, reliability, and truthfulness of that word. No generation, group, institution, church, or individual ever did anything significant for God if they also harbored lingering doubts about the effectiveness or the appropriateness of that word for the needs and issues at hand.

All tacit or even practical actions to the contrary must be renounced and our testimony must be the same as this widow's fine proclamation: "Now I know . . . that the word of God . . . is the truth." While many are rightfully concerned about junk food and malnutrition among the world's masses, where are those who are concerning themselves in prayer and action over the famine of the word of God — yes, sometimes even in the very midst of those churches that pride themselves on teaching and preaching the word of God? This word wants more from us than a mere mental assent or even a doctrinal affirmation; it wants a whole life of action and aspiration built on it for the honor and glory of the great name of our dependable and truthful Lord who has spoken to us in His Word.

THE WIDOW AND THE WORD

1 Kings 17:8-24

1. Is it improper to obtain personal comfort from the fact that God promised to keep the widow's flour and oil at a subsistence level until the famine was over? Can all people in all countries claim that same promise, or was it made here for a specific reason (without universal implications for the hunger problem)?

2. Have you ever had an experience in which you were running

"short" on food or money, yet you sensed God leading you to share what you had with someone in need? How did God bless you after you shared? How did He provide for you?

3. Just as God led the widow through an even greater trial after she trusted His word, so we often "pass one test" only to encounter a more severe one. Think of such a situation in your past, or in the life of a loved one. What did God teach you about His sovereignty? About the reliability of His word? About His love for you?

3

The Challenge
1 Kings 18:1-20

The story is told of a native American who witnessed for the first time the huge mushroom cloud created by a test atomic bomb blast. He is reported to have gasped, "I wish I would have said that!"

The story has an apocryphal ring to it, but the power which one of these blasts conjures up in any modern mind cannot be imaginary or contrived. It is a most awesome display of power.

What then shall we say about the power of God which produces even more awesome and wonderful effects — and this without any use of material means? To think that the mere announcement of the mighty word of God should be enough to rip open the order of events as we have been accustomed to experiencing them is breathtaking indeed.

It's too bad that our fondness for trivialities keeps us from experiencing the greatness, might and power of God. J. B. Phillips was on the right track when he complained some years ago that the God of most moderns was entirely too small. In fact, the greater God becomes in our hearts and minds, the smaller the crush of life's events and problems becomes in proportion to Him.

1 Kings 18 is a chapter where we meet ourselves, because we meet the power and greatness of the living God. The focal point of the chapter has to be verse 39 where the people, startled by the sudden appearance of the fire of God consuming everything on and around the altar built by Elijah, fell face-down to the ground and cried in stunned confession, "The LORD, he is God! The LORD, he is God!"

Now all this was done in order that all Israel (and we, too) might ". . . know that you, O LORD, are God and that you are turning their hearts back again" (verse 37). The knowledge spoken of here is not a cerebral or pure academic knowledge of God; instead, it is an experiential knowledge that comes from a whole-person involvement — the heart, the mind, the will, and the emotions.

WHAT IS GREATER THAN THE POWER OF GOD?

This chapter asks the same question of its original audience, and of us, that the magnificent fortieth chapter of Isaiah asks: "To whom then will you liken God or to what likeness will you compare Him?" In other words: *What now is the issue, problem, force, institution, political unit, or personal struggle that you feel is a match or even a greater power than the power of God the Lord?*

Even if we answer correctly on a doctrinal and conceptual level, the question still must be answered on a practical level, for it's all too possible to be correct in one's theology while continuing to act, think, and assume that in the real world different measures are needed.

More is needed than a mere doctrinal assent. We need to have a whole new demonstration of the mighty power of God in our times once again. The problem, of course, is not with God. We are the problem. Our experience of Christianity and of the militant program of God has grown all the more anemic and insipid.

The church all too often acts these days as if she were a wet noodle rather than a mighty army going out to do spiritual battle. Where is the demonstration of that power of the mighty

presence of the living Christ? Where is that practical application
of all the power of the resurrected Christ being seen in such
force that the powers of death, hell, and wickedness flee before
the face of His own?

The truth is that all too seldom have we seen it manifested
in any proportion to what the Lord of His church has wished
for us to experience. We need to experience a demonstration
of that power all over again — and 1 Kings 18 was put in the
Bible to help us witness how the demonstration of that power
operates when we meet God on His terms.

In what has to be one of the most breathtaking displays
of the power and majesty of God in the Old Testament, the
people on Mount Carmel were stirred as never before. What
a sight that must have been! I suppose it must have been
something like being at Cape Canaveral for the lift-off of one
of NASA's rockets into space. It makes a person shudder with
fright and dance with delight at the same time. What then
must these folks on Mount Carmel have thought — especially
when something like two million people were milling around
getting plenty bored after nine hours of no results due to the
antics of the fraudulent prophets of Baal. But then — a short
prayer, and *boom!* It was as if the sky blew apart and a huge
torch lit the altar with a heat so intense that everything was
charred to a crisp, including the stones, the water, dust, and all!

"LET THE FIRE FALL!"

Years ago, before we became conscious of ecology, tourists
at Yosemite Park were treated to a nightly display that never
failed to please the huge crowds that gathered to witness this
demonstration. High over the valley floor, the park rangers
would set a number of logs on fire and wait upstream near
one of those marvelous precipitous waterfalls that grace that
magnificent valley. When the hour of darkness had finally
arrived, the sonorous voice of a park ranger would ring out
from the valley floor: "Let the fire fall!"

Then the moment would come which all had waited so
patiently to witness; a hail of sparks and flames would appear
as the waters carried the burning logs over the brink of the
falls and down the steep descent of several hundred feet to
the valley floor and the waiting stream. The crowd loved it.
The fire fell along with the water. It appeared to happen as if

it were solely at the command of one man with a booming and demanding voice — as if he had some special contact with heaven itself.

If that is how it appeared to these campers in Yosemite Park, how must it have appeared to those somewhat skeptical Israelite fence-sitters who refused to adopt wholeheartedly Yahweh or Baal as their God? For just as surely as the park ranger called, "Let the fire fall," so this rustic from the backwoods area of Israel called to the living God. He did not rig his demonstration — this was the real thing. It was so real it was terrifying. Anything that would eat up rocks, dust, water, animals and all has got to be some sort of supernatural display.

Accordingly, God gives us three "demonstrations" of His power in 1 Kings 18. He demonstrates His power in His messenger (verses 1-20), in His actions (verses 21-40), and in His answers to prayer (verses 41-46).

NO FENCE-SITTING ALLOWED

He will do all of this so that Israel and we who now read this text may "know that the Lord, He is God." What this chapter despises and cannot stand more than anything else is fence-sitting — what politicians in another era called mugwumping (*i.e.*, people who sat on the political fence with their mug on one side and their you-know-what on the other side!).

Elijah challenged the people and demanded of them an answer to the same question our generation ought to be asked: "How long will you waver between two opinions? If the LORD is God, then follow Him; but if Baal is God, follow him" (verse 21).

Neither we nor Israel can expect to be able to live lives filled with power in a fence-sitting situation. Waffling back and forth (now depending on human sagacity, now on financial resources, now on political clout, now on some parliamentary ruse which others are unaware of), would eminently qualify for the opprobrium and disgrace that befalls all such half-hearted experiences of the power of God. Is that anything like the power of God encouraged in this chapter? Instead, it is so much like the world it is a crying shame to even connect all that nonsense with the mighty, powerful work of our sovereign God. It's time to cry, "Let the fire fall"; let poppycock and bosh cease in the church of the living and mighty God.

THE POWER OF GOD IN HIS MESSENGER

But let us take each of the three demonstrations in their
turn as they occur in this great eighteenth chapter of 1 Kings.
The first demonstration, which we'll discuss in this chapter,
can be seen in the power of God in his messenger Elijah
(verses 1-20).

What can the power of God do for me, you ask? Well,
just witness what it did for a man of rather ordinary abilities
like Elijah (James 5:17). He had every one of the emotions
and struggles that all of us have; yet look how bold and strong
he was. Is this because of some native skill or aptitude? Hardly,
for the context of this discussion is not about men, but about
knowing God and His power. Proverbs 28:1 hits the nail on
the head when it remarks, "The righteous are bold as a lion,
but the wicked flees when no one is chasing him."

Accordingly, God commanded His servant after three years
of waiting to "Go present yourself to Ahab" (verse 1). Elijah
is to walk right into the teeth of danger and confront his enemy
in his own den. This is an amazing command in that King
Ahab had by now exhausted every means known to man to
locate his nemesis. He had searched high and low throughout
the land of Israel. He had even sent to the neighboring countries
and required of them an oath that they had not seen Elijah
nor were they giving political asylum to him. If only Ahab
had known that Yahweh had provided for this servant right
under the nose of his father-in-law's domain in Sidon, he and
his miffed queen would have been furious.

It was against this background that God now ordered
Elijah to show up in broad daylight and to take on the king
on his own turf. In his fine book entitled *The Life of Elijah,*
A. W. Pink states the issue precisely: "Wicked men are generally
great cowards: their own consciences are their accusers, and
often cause them many misgivings when in the presence of
God's faithful servants, even though these occupy an inferior
position in life to themselves." He goes on to note that "Herod
feared John, knowing that he was a just and holy man" (Mark
6:20). "Felix trembled before Paul" even though Paul was the
prisoner and Felix was the Roman governor (Acts 24:25).[1]

The tragedy was that instead of letting the events of those
years soften their hearts, Ahab and Jezebel tried to "stonewall"

it with God. So infuriated was this dolled-up queen that she vented her wrath on the prophet-scholars of Jehovah and began killing them off. Meekly, the milk-toast Ahab, very much under the domination and sway of his power-hungry wife, fell into step with her deprogramming of Israel from the influence and worship of Yahweh.

HOW LONG WAS THE DROUGHT?

This command of God came "after many days." But how long after the events of chapter 17? 1 Kings 18:1 also says it was "in the third year." But this appears to be in conflict with Luke 4:25 and James 5:17, which give the figure of three and a half years. While some biblical scholars give the explanation that parts of a year count in the Hebrew system of reckoning (a fact which is, of course, amply illustrated elsewhere in the Old Testament), it is probably more accurate to take the prediction of 1 Kings 17:1 as coming approximately six months after the dry season has ended and when the rainy season had been expected under normal conditions. This way all of the statements are congruent. It is true that Jewish tradition maintains that the drought lasted only fourteen or eighteen months — an explanation which would interpret the three years as being parts of two years with a full year in between according to the Hebrew reckoning system seen elsewhere. We may never know which is the true explanation in this case until we have better evidence, but it would seem that the use of the figure of three and a half is most unusual for a figure of speech under the Hebrew reckoning system. One thing was for sure: It was all too long as far as the people and their government were concerned.

OBEDIENCE YIELDS RESULTS

There was a second half to that command God gave his servant in verse 1. He had directed, "Go and present yourself to Ahab," but then He added, "so that (or, in order that) I may send rain on the land." The connection of these clauses in Hebrew is more than the mere conjunction "and." There was an intimate connection to be observed between this act of obedience and the results that were to flow from it.

How important, then, are the very first steps of obedience. Without them, all would be impossible and unsuccessful. The

promise of God is not given on some new basis not otherwise
attested in Scripture. It is true that elsewhere we see a call
and positive response to repentance of the nation's sins as the
basis for the sending of the rain. The need for repentance of
the people was not being overlooked here even though we
have the two statements sitting side by side: "Go . . . and I
will send rain." The Spirit of God predicted that the rain would
come, but this was only putting things in an anticipatory light.
In fact, there must intervene between Elijah's going and the
coming of the rain:

1. a sacrifice for sin
2. the confession of the people
3. the further intercessory prayer of the prophet.

All of this was a long way from some kind of automatic
forgiveness and blessing without any intervening recognition
and dealing with the sin question.

"Now the famine was severe in Samaria," begins the
narrative in verse 2. Indeed it was, for the historian Josephus
also knew of a severe drought under the Syrian (our Phoenician)
King Ithobal (Ethbaal), a contemporary of Ahab.[2] But to what
use were the punishments of God? It was as Jeremiah would
later experience: "You, O LORD, struck them, but they were
not grieved; you crushed them, but they refused to repent"
(Jeremiah 5:3).

But God had his seven thousand who had not bowed the
knee to Baal, and He had his servant Obadiah, Ahab's sort of
Secretary of State. Of course the judgment of these days affected those who bowed the knee to Baal as well as it affected
the seven thousand. But while the drought and the resulting
famine were brought on by God, the persecution of the prophets
and the righteous (indeed of Elijah himself if Jezebel could
have gotten her slimy little hands on him) was only permitted
by God. Their blood was shed by wicked men under the aegis
of Jezebel's powers and authority. However, in this very act
of preserving a remnant, God was providing for a better day
when men and women would respond.

NOTHING CAN PREVAIL AGAINST GOD

No matter how violent and how vindictive the forces of

evil may appear on the surface of things and for the moment, they will never succeed against the power of the living Lord. Surely many a good prophet (we have no idea just how many) of Yahweh died at the brutal hands of this murderess; even as many have died under other despots. The evil leaders thought they had bested God in a contest of wills and power, yet none has ever succeeded — nor will they ever! They know very little about the power of God. Thus in our times neither communism nor Islam can hold a candle to the power of God. If only the church realized this in her mission of prayer and in her strategies for conquering the world for Christ, then every obstacle would fold up before her as if it were made of papier-mache.

Elijah's encounter with Obadiah was no chance meeting — not in a world where God's providence is constantly operating. What we know for sure about Obadiah is that "he feared the LORD greatly," (i.e., he was a most devout believer). Jewish tradition tries to equate him with the prophet by the same name who wrote the small book in the minor prophets or with the third captain of the band of fifty soldiers sent to bring Elijah back to the king in 2 Kings 1:13. Some even speculate that the widow of the prophet mentioned in 2 Kings 4:1-7 was his wife, but so much for speculation. This we do know: He was what his name indicated: "Servant of Yahweh." His own confession in verse 12 is that "I have feared (believed in) the LORD since my youth."

But what was he doing serving with such a vile king? How could such a man who feared God and who had walked devoutly with God since his youth have anything in common with Ahab? This had to be one of the major mismatches of history.

There is nothing wrong in holding a position of influence if it does not compromise one's principles and if one can render valuable service to the kingdom of God. Did not Daniel serve in several different political systems that were antithetical to the kingdom of God? And what shall we say of Joseph's service to Pharaoh? It would appear that we can sometimes draw our categories of separation from the world so tightly that they exceed the categories drawn from Scripture.

DID OBADIAH COMPROMISE HIS FAITH?

Some have complained that Obadiah was a compromiser

as exhibited by these features:

1. He showed no delight at seeing a fellow believer
2. He resented being told to tell Ahab that he was to go meet Elijah
3. He was self-centered and concerned only for his own position
4. He distrusted the words of Jehovah, lamely protesting that the Spirit of God would cart off Elijah after he went to tell Ahab that Elijah had returned
5. He was overly defensive, protesting that he had rescued one hundred prophets and served God since his youth.

But do all these features indicate a guilty conscience? I seriously doubt that this is true. Certainly, Obadiah was fearful, but he refers to natural fears, actual daring deeds, and to a real sincerity of heart and purpose even as the text affirms by telling us almost the identical information in verses 3 and 4. Thus we have here no vain boast, but a thoroughly attested case of genuine sincerity. The man was not without his faults, but he must not be judged solely by the position that he occupied in the government. While some may speculate that it would be difficult for him to steal away from his duties day after day and to supply food and water for some one hundred prophets of the Lord without some slight acquiescence from King Ahab, this is difficult to prove.

Thus the same providence of God that had previously prepared ravens and a Phoenician widow in a Sidonian suburb now also worked on the heart of a man within Israel to preserve two groups of fifty prophets. In all three cases it was God who made the instruments, called them into service and equipped them to carry out the task given to them. Therefore, we can likewise add that Obadiah did not receive his high position in Ahab's government acting independently of God's providence. The words that Mordecai spoke to Esther are just as *apropos* here: "Who knows? Perhaps you have come to the kingdom for such a time as this" (Esther 4:14).

THE CONFRONTATION BEGINS

The long-awaited confrontation between Ahab and Elijah finally took place, but the king had to walk to meet the prophet and not vice-versa. Ahab could only muster scorn and disdain for the one who had given him the word of the living God. Sneered Ahab, "Is that you, you troubler of Israel?" (verse 17).

How quick the wicked are to shift the blame from themselves and their own sins to those who merely serve as the messengers of that word! But just as the power of God could be observed in the prophet's rebuke of a fearful believer, Obadiah, so the power of God was now to be evidenced in the sharp rebuke this potentate in Israel would receive from one who on any other terms was regarded as a nobody.

The king's analysis of who or what was troubling Israel was deficient, to say the least. Elijah picked up on the exact term that the king had used and aimed the missile back to its sender. The only criterion that could reveal the source of the trouble was the one the king had so imperiously avoided: the covenant of God, especially as preserved in Deuteronomy 28. Had not verses 1-4 and 12 promised that God would give rain in its season on the land if they obeyed and walked in His way? And had not Deuteronomy 28:15,16, 18, and 22-24 warned that if they disobeyed the voice of the Lord, then the heavens over their heads would be turned to brass and the earth under their feet would become as hard as iron? So why all the flippant talk about "troublers of Israel?"

If the truth had been spoken, Ahab and Jezebel were more embarrassed over the non-performance of their celebrated deities of rain, thunder, dew, and fertility than they were over some idle threat of an unknown drifter from Gilead. It's embarrassing to have deities specializing in the "stuff" they cannot produce — not even for three and a half years. Baal did nothing — he sent no rain, no dew, no thunder. What an absolute flop, a disgrace to organized religion!

Ahab's smarting heart could manage no other rejoinder than to blame God's minister. But God's minister was fully in control. With the boldness that could only be another mark of the power of God, Elijah charged that the real troubler of Israel was none other than this leader, the king himself, and his family. It was their abandonment of the word of God that had brought this proud nation to such a sorry state of affairs. "To be precise, O King, it was your worship of the various Baals that was the reason for the mess we are in," announced Elijah.

Now that is telling it like it is! No fancy footwork that

dances around the point without coming right out with the real goods. The king was left without a leg to stand on. Troubler of Israel, indeed — it is you, O King!

THE CHALLENGE

Thoroughly rebuffed and completely reduced in the presence of the mighty, convicting word of God, Ahab was in no shape to issue any ringing indictments of his own or to command that God's servant be bound. Instead, Elijah seized the initiative and delivered his own denouement: "Now summon the people from all over Israel to meet me on Mount Carmel. And bring the four hundred and fifty prophets of Baal and the four hundred prophets of Asherah, who eat at Jezebel's table" (verse 19).

Wow! Would a king stand for this? To be ordered around like this? Who is king here anyhow? Isn't the prophet exceeding his authority?

What was Ahab to do? He needed water and he needed it badly. If this was the only way to get water, then so be it; he was beyond being embarrassed by the niceties of diplomacy and the rights of the throne to say what would or would not happen and when. He was a desperate man. Moreover, "The king's heart is in the hand of the Lord" (Proverbs 21:1).

Eight hundred and fifty against one! That hardly seems fair. But when the powerful God of the universe is on your side, you've got the majority. The big showdown on Mount Carmel was about to begin!

THE CHALLENGE
1 Kings 18:1-20
1. Was Obadiah, Ahab's Secretary of State, a devout or a compromising believer? In what ways can we Christians be intimidated by our society? What spiritual resources are available to us as believers to meet these challenges?
2. Read James 5:13-18. Did Elijah have any special powers or pedigree to warrant God's favor? Why do you suppose God was able to display His power through Elijah? What does this tell you about your walk with God today?
3. Can you think of any power which is greater than the power of God? What does this mean to you today, in the particular challenges and trials you are facing at this moment?

4

The Big Showdown
1 Kings 18:21-46

God delights in taking people who may or may not have accomplished something and making these people into mighty channels of His power and might when they act in accordance with all that He has spoken in His Word. These people are still in high demand today. There is much talk today about "high tech and high touch." What God wants is "high trust and light touch."

This mighty power can be demonstrated in more than the lives of His servants; it can also be seen in the action of life. A second time in 1 Kings 18 God vindicated Himself, but this time in one of the most sensational challenges ever witnessed by mortals anywhere — except for the resurrection of Jesus Christ from the dead. Verses 20-40 record this marvelous showdown on Mount Carmel. It is filled with awe and humorous sidelights along the way.

Ahab meekly complied with the edict laid down by God's man Elijah. I wonder if Ahab consulted Jezebel first, or if he was too frightened to face her with the fact that he had caved in before his chief enemy. Strange, isn't it, that Jezebel was not present for this gala event?

When all the people and the false prophets of Israel had assembled on this mountain on which the waves of the Mediterranean Sea lapped, Elijah got right down to business. Standing before the people, he demanded, "How long will you go limping between two opinions? If the Lord is God, then serve him; but if Baal is God, follow him" (verse 21). That was the issue: two parties, two opinions, two minds, two loyalties. It would never work. The psalmist spoke plainly: "I hate [says the Lord] double-minded men" (Psalm 119:113).

The word we have translated here as "limping" is the picture of people walking as if they were intoxicated. They were walking with a swagger, not uprightly, and therefore were fickle and inconstant. But it was time to stop all this nonsense and come to a definite decision.

WE MUST TAKE A STAND

Our day has been marked by a very similar eclecticism. It is almost as if everyone has a small piece of religious truth, and the object of the game is not to be too dogmatic about any one option in the religious arena lest one should cut himself off from some very insightful contributions. But where are the discerning individuals who will stand up and confess with Joshua, "But as for me and my house, we will serve the LORD" (Joshua 24:15). Did not Jesus say, "He that is not with me is against Me" (Matthew 12:30)? Did not the Lord of the church at Laodicea warn that "I would that you were cold or hot" (Revelation 3:15)? But since they were just lukewarm, He would spit them out of His mouth. Lukewarmness is a blending type of action in which the Laodiceans were also attempting to straddle the fence. But it does not work.

The question was and still is, "Who is on the LORD'S side? Let him come to Me" (Exodus 32:26). The incident at the golden calf was not all that different from this event as well. A choice had to be made. No man or woman could serve two masters.

So what did the people say to this? These certainly were serious charges and no one was going to stand there and just take that kind of talk — unless that talk was clearly a manifestation of the power of God. And it was, for "the people said nothing."

Says A. W. Pink wistfully, "O for that plain and faithful preaching which would so reveal to men [and women] the unreasonableness of their position . . . that every objection would be silenced and they would stand self-condemned."[1]

After the people had assembled, the terms of the contest were set by God's prophet. The god that answered by fire would be declared to be the only true and legitimate deity.

WHY FIRE INSTEAD OF WATER?

But why fire? I should think that things were hot enough after all these months of drought and scorching sun. What everyone longed for more than anything else was rain and water; so why should they call for fire? The answer to this most proper question uncovers the heart of the theological matter at hand. Not only would the flaming descent of fire show the power of God, but more importantly at this point, it would clearly announce the fact that there had to be an acceptance of a sacrifice to intervene before there could be any blessing of rain, dew, or the like.

There was even more to it than that. The fire must come of itself from heaven and therefore signify that God had been propitiated. Indeed, the sacrifice itself would speak of a substitute that would bear the sins of the people and thereby make possible the forgiveness and subsequent blessing of God. God could not forgive without someone, either in reality or in pictorial promise, paying for the sin of the people. It is impossible to forgive anyone without someone paying — even on the human level. That is why we are so loathe to forgive one another. In this case, Elijah placed the bull on the altar and waited for heaven itself to be the officiating priest.

This was only the fourth time in Israel's history that fire had fallen from heaven. The first was when the tabernacle was built and the first sacrifice was put in place. God let fire fall from heaven to ignite that first offering and thereby He approved of the whole order of things connected with the tabernacle and its sacrifices (Leviticus 9:24). The second instance was when David obtained the site for the future temple and built the first altar on the spot; fire fell once again (1 Chronicles 21:26). This was repeated when Solomon finished the temple and fire again fell as a sign of its acceptance and approval by God (2 Chronicles 7:1).

The Mount Carmel showdown was to be the fourth time.

Since the prophets of Baal were more numerous, Elijah urged that they go first. They chose one of the bulls and began their acts of religious devotion to Baal. But this was to turn into a real marathon: from early morning to mid-afternoon. There certainly was no lack of fervor or ardor; these devotees did everything they could to attract the attention of their erstwhile non-existent deity.

ELIJAH ENJOYS THE SHOWDOWN

One would think that Elijah would be somewhat nervous and moody as he reflected on the fact that his turn was coming up soon. What had he gotten himself into? But no — Elijah was as loose and relaxed as a man on vacation. What did he have to fear? Had not God fed him by the ravens? Hadn't God directed him to a gentile town and miraculously replenished a depleted supply of oil and flour? Had Elijah not seen the dead raised back to life? So what fear or anxiety should now possess his soul over such a small matter as getting God to answer by fire from heaven? He had seen the power of God, and once you have seen the power of God all else is child's play.

In fact, Elijah was so relaxed that he began to offer help to somewhat beleaguered and befuddled members of the local prophetic guild. If you have never smiled when you were reading Scripture, this is the appropriate place. I picture the prophet in a totally relaxed position waiting for these religious robots to exhaust themselves. Could it be that he used the time to sun himself on the hillside, casually chewing on a piece of straw? Regardless, he did begin to have heaps of fun at their expense. He suggested that they shout louder; the hard-pressed idolaters accepted the suggestion and increased the volume. By now their hobgoblin prancing with its charac-teristic weapons-dance had turned into a most bloody and despicable scene. In an effort to attract the notice of Baal, the prophets shed their own blood as they masochistically beat on their own backs hoping that the sacred blood of dedicated priests and prophets would merit special attention from the gods. But there were no gods home: What was the use of all the trouble?

Elijah came to the rescue again as he jeered, "Shout louder, for Baal may be sleeping! Maybe he's out of town! Perhaps he can't come to the phone right now!" The prophet was having loads of fun — and so he should after all he had been through. He had waited and prayed so long because these charlatans had robbed Israel of their rightful experience of the fellowship and blessing of God. Smile, Elijah, and rejoice, for your sarcasm is justified. The emptiness and falsity of the whole charade must now be exposed under the white heat of God's truth.

EXPOSING THE CHARADE

This buffoonery continued past midday. At the time of the evening sacrifice, about 3 P.M., Elijah had had enough. He signaled that it was his turn and that these religious con artists should now admit defeat. Elijah summoned the people to draw in closer, for he wanted them to be sure they were not missing anything, either in the preparation or in the pending effects.

He then took twelve stones, one for each of the twelve tribes of Israel, and remade the altar that by now had been reduced to shambles by the antics of 850 crazed prophets. But why *twelve* stones? This was the north and there were only ten tribes recognized up here. But the prophet would have none of these petty arguments, for what God established in the covenant was good enough for him.

Even more significantly, as Elijah set up the twelve stones, he said, "Your name shall be Israel" (verse 31). That was a deliberate reference to the informing theology from Genesis 35:2,10-12. There God had told Jacob long ago to "Get rid of your foreign gods . . . your name shall be called Israel, not Jacob." Thus the point was clearly made: Israel had been in this same type of trouble once before. Their very name was to be a reminder of the previous time they dropped this lunacy of serving other gods. Alas, what she learned was what all of us learn too late: The past is forgotten, only to be repeated by those who will not remember it.

Elijah's restoration of the altar was also of significance, for the now-divided nation was in itself another reminder of sin in their midst. The building of an altar usually marked the spot where God revealed His name (Exodus 20:24) and would be no less true here as well.

Just before Elijah prayed for the fire to descend, he did something which seemed very strange. He ordered that everything be drenched with water. This was done not only once, but three times. Some protest that this was impossible since there was a water shortage. But they had the waves of the Mediterranean Sea lapping at the base of the very mountain they were on, and it made little difference whether it was salt water or not.

Many of us today are especially glad that Elijah followed this procedure, for we are sure that had it not been done, there would have been numerous doctoral theses and scholarly tomes suggesting that the fire was the result of some latent spontaneous combustion from the sparks left by the swords that the Baal and Asherah prophets had used when they had taken their frenzied turn just minutes before Elijah. This, along with the hot and late afternoon sun, did its work and Elijah was fortunate enough to have been the recipient of all their hard work!

But that theory, fortunately for the sake of our already-overtaxed apologetical skills, is all wet. Elijah made sure of it. The soaking received by the altar, the bull, the wood, and the trench is clearly indicated in the text.

HEAVEN'S FIREFALL

At the same moment that the evening sacrifice was being celebrated in downtown Jerusalem, one lonely man (plus the Almighty God) stood up on Mount Carmel and prayed a very simple prayer of approximately sixty words. His appeal was to the God of the fathers of that country, Abraham, Isaac, and Israel (recall Genesis 35). His motivation was simply that God would be known in Israel and that the people would know that He indeed was God.

Then the fire fell — only this was more dramatic and breath-taking than it was in Yosemite Park. It is called the "fire of Yahweh" (verse 38). It consumed everything: the wood, the sacrifice, the stones, the dust, and the water. No wonder the people fell on their faces and cried, "The LORD — He is God!" (verse 39). And well they should. What a mighty God we worship!

The prayer of Elijah never faltered. There is no record that he peeked to see if there were any signs of smoke or fire.

There is no record that he protracted his prayer and began to pray around the world for all the missionaries and whatever else he could think of in an effort to stall in case God would not be able to answer his request. He prayed confidently and with full expectation that he would be heard and that God would intervene as He had promised.

The preparation for this prayer was not accomplished in one lovely afternoon's sunbath out on the lovely site of Mount Carmel. No, Elijah had prepared for this moment in three long years of intimate, obedient fellowship with God.

PRAYER AND THE POWER OF GOD

Prayer is the third and final demonstration of the power of God seen in 1 Kings 18. Not only do we see Elijah in public prayer on the Mount, but now in the last verses of this chapter (40-46), we see him in private prayer.

But why, you ask, must he now pray for rain since God already gave him a firm promise in 1 Kings 18:1 that He would send rain? That is just the point this text wishes to make about prayer and the power of prayer. The promises of God are not meant to exempt us from the ministry and hard work of praying; rather, they are given to us in order to teach us what it is we ought to pray for!

It is no wonder that James 5:17 cites Elijah as an example of prayer. Notice that he:

1. withdrew from the crowd
2. prostrated himself in the attitude and posture of prayer
3. based his prayer on the promises of God
4. was fervent in his praying
5. was watchful in the course of his praying
6. was definite in what he prayed for.

Even though he had been promised by God that if he would present himself to Ahab, God would send rain, Elijah still entered wholeheartedly into the work of prayer and he refused to give up until there were definite signs that the answer was now on the way.

Some readers balk at Elijah's command ordering the people to "seize the prophets of Baal and let none escape" (verse 40). But if every Israelite who served an idol deserved to be stoned to death (Deuteronomy 17:5), then what must the judgment of God be for those who had *sponsored* this aberration in Israel? That judgment was spelled out in the same word of God that issued the covenant the people had also bypassed. Prophets who said, "Let us go and serve other gods" were dealt with severely (Deuteronomy 13:13).

Strange, isn't it, that our generation has trouble making such judgments on those who send men to an eternity of damnation forever, but our generation has no trouble being stirred to the limit over some doctors or terrorists who cause a temporal death which lasts only until the Lord returns! Both, of course, are downright revolting; but only the physical form of wrong earns our justified wrath. This too tells us more about ourselves than it does about the legitimacy of this command.

RAIN AND REJOICING

And the rains came and great was the rejoicing of the people who had all but given up any hope of ever seeing rain again. With delight Elijah raced ahead of Ahab's chariot all the way across the famous plain of Meggido to the northern king's summer palace at Jezreel — a trip of some eighteen miles! The power of God is the only reason given for this tremendous feat, and this final note captures the essence of the whole chapter. The prophet, with great hopes, accompanied the king on foot — not as a proof of his humility, nor as a personal bodyguard to rescue him from the angry crowd that might have felt betrayed by his leading them into idolatry; no, it was perhaps a further offer to stand by King Ahab in hopes that the king's conscience might be stirred to godly living and that he might then help to counter the malicious effects of Jezebel's refusal to accept this great work of God.

WHAT ELSE REALLY MATTERS?

Who then is a God like our God? May all the people shout as they did on Mount Carmel, "The LORD, He is God. The LORD — He is God." Our generation needs this kind of display of the power of God in men and women, in the work of God around the globe, and in the most vital ministry of prayer.

If God has slipped in our esteem, then we need to come to Him with confession and a prayer that He would visit us with His power once again. He is the one who can shatter our neat and traditional categories. Even the strongholds of evil and false systems are no match for His great power. So why do we stand gazing out over the times or staring at one another when our gaze ought to be focused on our powerful Lord? The day will soon come when every knee shall bow and every tongue confess that He is Lord and that there is nothing else that matters in the whole world.

So why don't we begin right now?

THE BIG SHOWDOWN
1 Kings 18:21-46

1. What would be a good contemporary definition of idolatry if we were to judge it by the forms it takes today? What is the best way to deal with these modern forms of idolatry so that the power of the living Lord may still be evidenced in our day?

2. What is a proper view of the Christian's right to expect miracles in our day? Are there any guidelines or limits on what we may or may not legitimately expect God to do without at the same time demeaning His power?

3. What requests should be the rightful objects of a believer's prayer? At what point do we exceed the limits of zeal and cross over into praying that our own will be done, all in the name of the mighty power of God?

4. What was Elijah's long-term preparation for his showdown/ prayer on Mount Carmel? What does this say to us about our ongoing "preparation" for prayers of faith?

5

"How Can I Serve God When I'm So Discouraged?"
1 Kings 19:1-8

Did you ever have someone ask you in an accusing manner, "What are you doing here?"

Perhaps it was when you were a child, or during a time of emergency when certain areas of the country or parts of the plant at work were restricted. In these days of tight airport security, that question will come quickly if any of us as unauthorized persons move out on the airport tarmac without proper identification and authorization. Surely we will be greeted with an imperious sounding voice, "*What* are you doing here?"

Think then how pointed that question sounded to Elijah as God twice directed it to him in verses 9 and 13 of 1 Kings 19. In a way they help us to get at the writer's main point in this chapter. The transition from chapter 18 to chapter 19 is sudden, strange, and unexpected: In the scope of just one or two verses and in the space of just one day, we go from the heights of Mount Carmel and the grandest day on which God has ever answered a mortal man's prayer, to the depths of the barren desert outside Beersheba almost ninety miles south with the same prophet thoroughly demoralized and drained of all spiritual zest, fervor and power.

No wonder the insistent question intrudes into the brooding prophet's moment of self-pity and disgrace: "What are you doing here, Elijah?"

FROM THE PINNACLE TO THE PITS

The exhilaration of the previous day's success suddenly disappeared and now God's servant despaired to the degree that he lost all taste for life itself. That situation is not all that unique, unfortunately. Frequently we, too, have plunged from tremendous heights where we experienced the power and spiritual energy of the living God, down to the depths of despair.

Without trying to make these men norms for our own situations or even to use them as excuses for failing to draw on the rich presence and power of God, we can note several other biblical characters who also fell into the same sandtraps of life.

Who can forget the events that Jonah went through? When he was prophesying of the expansion of the kingdom of God and the success of Israel (2 Kings 14:25), he was in his element. But when the assignment came to go and preach to Israel's archenemy, the Assyrians in their capital of Nineveh, he decided that it was time to take a vacation in sunny Spain (Tarshish). It was only after his harrowing experience at sea that he began to realize that a man can't just resign from God's service. Before it was all over, Jonah would really know what it was like to be down in the mouth.

Baruch, Jeremiah's secretary, likewise went through a similar feeling of deep discouragement and frustration. In Jeremiah 45:3 he despaired, "Woe is me! . . . I am worn out with groaning and find no rest." He had just faced the bitterest disappointment of his life in the fact that others achieved success and had something to show for their lives and all their work. His brother, for example, had been appointed as the king's staff officer (Jeremiah 51:59) but he was merely the secretary of the prophet Jeremiah. He had spent all his life writing this Book of Jeremiah only to have the impudent king take his infamous penknife out and cut his manuscript up piece by piece and consign it to the fire in the hall where this work was being read to him (Jeremiah 36 — Note the dateline on that chapter and the dateline in chapter 45). God's rebuke to his prophet was this: "Should you seek great things for yourself? Seek them not" (Jeremiah 45:5). In fact, God said, in effect: "If you think you have troubles, then consider My position; what I have built up in Israel over this last millennia and a half I must now disassemble and pull down because of the people's sin." The times were too serious for any sulking about what should or should not have happened.

The depression such men experienced was all easily understandable — and from their viewpoint natural enough; but it was not natural from God's viewpoint. All too frequently our experience is like that of the psalmist: "[We] mount up to the heaven, [we] go down to the depths; in peril [our] courage melts away . . . [we] are at our wits' end. Then [we] cry out to the Lord in [our] troubles and He brings [us] out of [our] distresses" (Psalm 107:26-28 — I have changed the pronouns from third person to first person in order to emphasize the personal application).

HOPE FOR THE DESPERATE MOMENTS

"What then are we doing here?" That is the question of this chapter. Our hopes, our dreams, our "could-have-beens," our heart-desires sometimes lie shattered at our feet. At such moments a terrific sense of frustration and despair begins to set in. God appears to be hidden or unconcerned with our deep sense of loss.

It is for times like these that 1 Kings 19 was written. For such situations, when we know intellectually that the word of God is dependable and that the power of Christ is more than available, God sends His special cures for all such beleaguered men and women. They are:

1. proofs of His love (1 Kings 19:1-8)
2. signs of His goodness (verses 9-14)
3. a fresh call to service (verses 15-21).

In this chapter, we'll look closely at three tangible proofs of His love to one who was wallowing in despair.

The Scripture is unique among the religious literature of the world in that it paints its characters in their true colors.

Never does the text attempt to gloss over these men and women and make them into plaster saints. There they stand with warts, blemishes and all. But the text is not about the men and the women; it is about our gracious God. Thus chapter 19 focuses on Him once again just as chapters 17 and 18 have. In this way, we are spared the embarrassment of incorrectly making the lives and actions of the text's characters into a normative line of acting or thinking when all the time it is God and His word that is the only worthwhile and authoritative teaching being commended in the text.

JEZEBEL STRIKES BACK . . .

Immediately after Mount Carmel, everything was going well for the prophet who had waited and prayed so long for this moment. *Surely,* he must have thought, *now the revival will begin.* Had not the people just bowed in unison and in deep acknowledgment that "the LORD, He is God; the LORD — He is God"? Now Israel's loose reign of wickedness and idolatry surely would come to an abrupt halt. Elijah could hardly wait for the reaction of the court. Certainly, King Ahab would now lead this nation in a new crusade for godliness and righteousness.

So Elijah had hoped. But the factor he had not reckoned with was Queen Jezebel.

When Ahab returned from his all-day affair on Mount Carmel and began to relate in undoubtedly excited tones "everything Elijah had done," Jezebel was not impressed. On the contrary, she became downright furious when she heard the punch line: "He [has] killed all the prophets with the sword." That did it. No one was going to trifle with Queen Jezebel and her special religious cronies! Never mind all this trite talk about fire from heaven, and who cared whether Baalism was true. They were *her* prophets and this was an attack on *her* religion. Elijah had embarrassed *her* gods; he would have to answer to *her* for this. What poor Ahab thought about all of this we can only guess, but I am sure he at least uttered an exasperated, hen-pecked sigh.

Jezebel's tactic was extremely clever: She sent a messenger to Elijah, who must have been resting out in the palace garden overlooking that beautiful plain of Esdraelon, and announced with an oath that the queen would take his life on the morrow just as he had taken the lives of her prophets. But this was a strange threat. Why not take his life immediately, if she was all that hot and bothered? What was the point in letting him live until the next day?

Therein we see the shrewdness of this woman. Jezebel was too bright to have Elijah executed on the same day in which his popularity was riding so high. There were still too many people around who had witnessed the great events on Mount Carmel and who now genuinely believed that this man was a bonafide prophet of Yahweh. Futhermore, it would not be too healthy a thing to do to infuriate this fickle crowd, for already in fifty-eight years, more than a few of the seven kings in the northern empire had been murdered. There was no sense in getting killed by this crowd.

Jezebel's wrath was not stirred simply by the unexpected turn of events; she was reacting to the pointed revelation of Yahweh in her life. The failure of her gods and prophets was a stinging indictment of all that was false, artificial, contrived, and worthless in her life. Meanwhile, like the blazing flash of fire from heaven, God had decisively spoken His mind to her and to all who limped along in this type of foolishness.

. . . AND ELIJAH HITS THE ROAD

With cunning skill, Jezebel decided to intimidate her opponent and to strike fear into his heart. If Elijah could be scared off, this would be more effective in reducing his heroic status in the eyes of the people than killing him and making a martyr out of him. It was a risky gamble, but as it worked out, her hunch paid off. She was able to restore part of her badly tarnished image and the land was temporarily rid of this nuisance.

To make it all sound tough, she uttered her pronouncement with an oath sworn by her gods. She cleverly tried to neutralize her oath by deleting the little word "me" from the oath (in the original Hebrew; the translations usually add it for the purposes of making sense to the English reader). But what did she have to lose with such worthless deities who already had been exposed as frauds? The amazing thing is that the human heart, convinced against its will of error, still clings to error in spite of all the evidences to the contrary.

The hoax worked. Verse 3 says, "Elijah was afraid and

he ran for his life." But why should Elijah be afraid? After his triumphant experience, you'd think he would have warned this haughty, domineering manipulator that she had better watch out who she was threatening. Did she wish to be smitten with fire from on high? Would she personally like to see the same power of God who had answered by fire on Carmel? This was no time to back down. The word of God would be blemished. This woman was a mere toy compared to the almighty power of God and the force that lay at the prophet's fingertips.

Nevertheless, Elijah was spooked by her verbiage and he left the field of battle in disappointment and disarray. The text says that "he ran for his life." C. F. Keil tries to aid poor Elijah by placing a spiritual construction on these words. In Keil's view, the fact that Elijah retreated to nearby Judah, then on to Beersheba and eventually Mount Horeb or Sinai is an indication that he went there for spiritual refreshment — for R & R. In other words, Keil translates this phrase this way: "He ran for his *soul.*"[1]

But this hardly seems to match the situation. Elijah was in no mood to be going on a spiritual retreat. It is true that his words appear to be contradictory, but then so were his emotions; they blew this way and that in his deep state of confusion, frustration and loneliness.

Thus the enemy had found his weak spot. Facing up to the odds of some 850 false prophets, being fed by ravens, praying that God would answer by fire, and even raising the dead were no major problems for this man of faith; but the threats of one woman — that was something different!

FAILING IN THE AREA OF YOUR STRENGTH

This should warn us against glorifying the individual rather than God. It also should warn us that many fail in the very area of their strengths. For example, Abraham was a man of faith, yet he lied to Pharaoh about his wife Sarah in order to preserve what he could not preserve unless God preserved it. Moses, likewise, was a man noted for his meekness, yet he spoke unadvisedly with his lips when he had had about enough from the murmuring Israelites. John was the apostle of love and yet he and James wanted to call down fire on the Samaritans when they failed to believe Jesus. In the same manner Elijah was renowned for his boldness, courage and power, but he too, failed in the very area of his strength. His courage and boldness melted away.

How frequently the Bible must warn us against fear. However, there are two different uses of fear in the Scriptures. These are best observed in Exodus 20:20, where Moses cautioned, "Fear not . . . only, fear the LORD." The first "fear" is the paralyzing phenomenon of being frightened and scared. This can cripple a person's effectiveness and grant the enemy a decided edge in almost any circumstance. But the second "fear" is a positive attitude of trust and commitment in the Lord Himself. That is the only sure way to prevent such a debacle as the one Elijah got himself into. Isaiah 8:12,13 encourages us by saying, "Do not fear what they fear . . . The LORD of hosts is the one you are to regard as holy; He is the one you are to fear, He is the one you are to dread."

THE NEGATIVE WITNESS OF FEAR

Elijah should not have feared or fled. His flight was the result of his unbelief and his failure to trust God in one more small-but-important moment of life. That is why the Lord insisted on pressing the question: "What are you doing here, Elijah?" By fleeing, Elijah as much as confessed before Jezebel and all her cohorts that the power of the kingdom of darkness was greater than the power of the kingdom of God's dear Son.

It appears that Elijah dismissed his servant at this point. His frame of mind was so morose that he began to despair of life itself. "It is enough," he mourned from under the broom tree. This desert shrub, which rarely grows more than ten feet high and affords a minimum of shade because of its thin branches and small leaves, would serve him well as his final resting spot on this earth. "I've had it," Elijah was moping. "I've lived long enough; I'm no better than my forefathers. Take my life."

But how could this be? If he wanted to surrender his life for the Lord, he should have stayed around Jezreel: Jezebel would have gladly obliged him. He must have been testing God, pretending that he was ready to die; yet he had just fled the scene of his calling in order to protect his life. Was this merely a case of the "poor me's"? Or did God's servant have a genuine case of depression? From our viewpoint, it is difficult to say. Furthermore, we must resist again the temptation to concentrate on the man rather than on God Himself. Accordingly, those who reverse this focus end up either praising the prophet by pointing out that he was not afraid to die, or trying to derive some Christological message from the fact that he must have been alone just as Christ was alone in the days of His humiliation.

His request for death is not to be equated with the apostle Paul's "desire to depart and to be with Christ which is far better" (Philippians 1:23). It is more like Jonah's complaint: "Take my life; it's better for me to die than to live" (Jonah 4:3). Or like Moses's jeremiad: "I can't take this people any longer . . . Put me to death . . ." (Numbers 11:14,15). Elijah simply turned peevish and petulant after being frustrated in his deep desire to see something happen for the glory of God.

THREE PROOFS OF GOD'S LOVE

If these verses describe the patient and his needs, verses 5-9 describe the proofs of God's love for His disheartened servant. These proofs in no way condone the fact that His servant has left the field of service; they do show the love of God in contrast to the faithlessness of His servant.

First of all, God gave sleep to His beloved — not a small item considering the amount of energy put out at the Mount Carmel site, the eighteen-mile marathon run back to Jezreel and now the seventy-five mile hike to the desert of Beersheba. What Elijah needed more than anything else was refreshment to rest his jangled nerves and exhausted body. He also had to be renewed for the long journey down to Mount Sinai.

A second proof of God's love: He sent a ministering angel to wait on Elijah. This time God did not use ravens; He did the task Himself, yes, even for a sinning and disappointing man. Verse 5 says it was "an angel," but verse 7 makes it clear that this was nothing less than a Christophony (i.e., an appearance of the second person of the Trinity) who was called "the Angel of the Lord." Since no angels had appeared to Elijah previously, you ask, why do any appear to him now? Is this a sign that God approved of His servant's sin?

Hardly. Christ Himself came to minister to His distraught and disorganized servant as a special proof of His love. This love was needed to soften His servant's smarting and disturbed heart. In a similar way, Hebrews 1:14 tells us, God continues to send forth His ministering spirits, or regular angels, to serve those who will inherit salvation.

Therefore, just as it was an angel who shut the lion's mouth in Daniel 6:2; an angel who delivered Lot from Sodom in Genesis 19:15,16; an angel who loosed Peter's chains and opened the iron city gate in Acts 12:7,10; and an angel who told Paul that no one on board the shipwrecked vessel would lose their lives if they stayed with the ship until Paul signaled otherwise (Acts 17:23); so it was an angel here, too — only this angel was an appearance of Christ!

It was a fairly common matter to have Christ appear in the Old Testament in His pre-incarnate form as "the Angel of the Lord." Thus, just as the Lord sent His angel ahead of the Israelites in the wilderness journey — an angel indeed in whom He had placed His name — so He sent His angel ahead of Elijah before he began his forty-day trip from Beersheba down to Mount Sinai — a trip Deuteronomy 1:2 tells us would normally be a trip of eleven days for a nation with children and all its herds and belongings.

GOD'S MINISTRY OF ANGELS

Believers would be well advised to thank God for the ministry of His angels, for many a time we have been in harm's way and we did not know it, but our angel did and He delivered us — thanks be to God. Here, the supreme one Himself, our Lord Jesus, appeared as an angel and put on the towel of service as He personally waited on His disheartened prophet.

The third proof of God's love was to be found in His provision of physical sustenance for Elijah. In the unwearied love of God, He bid His servant to wake up a second time and to receive food. While the meal was simple, it had its luxuries. It was prepared hot right at his side (almost like a Japanese hibachi meal cooked at the table) with a jar of water — all this out in the desert!

After Elijah had received such tender care, he got up and began his journey to Sinai. The forty-day journey, as we have already noted, is excessively long, unless God providentially allowed him to drag the journey out and thus symbolically recall the forty years of Israel's wanderings in the wilderness. If so, then Elijah could not help but be reminded of Israel's sin as well as the faithfulness of God. Is that what he was being reminded of as God prepared him for the reenlistment ceremony He had in store for him? I believe so. Once more, grace was prevailing in the revelation of the Old Testament.

ELIJAH, DISCOURAGEMENT, AND YOU

1 Kings 19:1-8

1. Think of a time in your life when a period of elation was soon followed by discouragement and depression. What do you think caused such a dramatic emotional swing in your life? How did God minister to you during that time of need?
2. Why do you think Elijah fled the scene in fear after he had just witnessed such a dramatic display of God's power?
3. Review the examples in this chapter of how many believers inadvertently fail in the area of their strengths. Reflect on your own spiritual strengths . . . how might you also fail, if you're not walking in the power of God's Spirit?
4. Review the discussion of the two types of fear observed in Exodus 20:20. Think of specific incidents in your life when (a) the first type of fear paralyzed you, and (b) the second type of fear freed you. What specific strategies will you employ to maintain a "healthy" fear when circumstances frighten you?

6

Turning Defeat Into Determination
1 Kings 19:9-21

When Elijah finally arrived at Sinai, he was directed to "*the* cave" (verse 9). Now that is strange, for no cave has been mentioned thus far in the text, but the Hebrew text specifically uses the article with the word *cave*. The only cave this can refer to is the one mentioned in Exodus 33:12 where Moses was sheltered "in the cleft of the rock." In addition to this, that is the place where God promised "to cause to pass by all my goodness" (Exodus 33:19). That is a second reason for connecting these two passages, for in 1 Kings 19:11 the Lord promised once again to "pass by."

At the very cave where God had revealed all His glory to Moses, God now asked Elijah why he had abandoned the field of service. The prophet was more than happy to answer that question; he knew why he was there. It was because of his thorough disillusionment with God's people. They were covenant breakers, that's what they were. And worse still, they had broken down the altars of the Lord. This surely meant that they wished for the way to God to be blocked. They no longer wished to follow Him or the dictates of His will. Unfortunately, when the way to God is blocked, God's way to man can also be blocked by the same act. The real blow, however, was the fact that the prophets had also been murdered in order to block their ministry of the word which would disturb the people's consciences. Only darkness can follow the blanking out of the word of God. No wonder the prophet complained!

But then if all this were true, and it does appear that Elijah's claim could be easily substantiated, why was God's prophet so far afield from where he was needed and where he had been sent? That is the Lord's question. Elijah reminds us of that familiar scene where a father is trying to discipline a son, only to have the son say, "What about them? What are you going to do about them?"

ELIJAH FEELS USELESS

There is another aspect to this answer: Elijah felt useless. He had been extremely zealous for the Lord, but there seemed to be no one else who cared. There is no word about the one hundred prophets of Yahweh that Obadiah had preserved alive during Jezebel's harrowing purge. Where had they gone? Had Elijah temporarily forgotten about them? Or had some mischief overtaken them?

The language of Elijah's complaint to God about his zealousness for God's work is taken from the Lord's description of Phineas's "jealousy" for the Lord in Numbers 25:11-13. Could it be that Elijah wished to remind God of how He had approved of Phineas and that He had rewarded him, but in the meantime Elijah seemed to be getting the wrong end of each deal?

There was no sudden rebuke from heaven which shouted in rebuttal, "Wrong! I have seven thousand who have not bowed the knee to Baal, so forget all this self-pity talk!" Instead, Elijah was told to go out and stand on the mountain in the presence of God. That appears to be a full circle back to 1 Kings 17:1 where he told Ahab that he was more aware of standing in the presence of God than he was of standing in the presence of the king of Israel. Is this what God wanted Elijah to recall? Had Elijah forgotten the power that is to be found in the constant recollection that we stand and serve in the presence of the living God? If he had, he would certainly get a good refresher course immediately, for God was just about ready to pass by and this man would once again see all the goodness of God. Seeing the goodness and greatness of God can make all the problems of life shrink to their proper size.

But first there would be an acted-out parable. Three signs that traditionally accompany the presence of God in theophanies throughout the Old Testament were suddenly invoked by God as this natural parable began just outside the cave where Elijah had been led to regain his perspective on life.

First there was a tornado with such obvious force and violence that it must have ripped the rocks from their natural ledges and tossed them about the valley floor as if they were mere seeds being blown in the wind. Trouble was, God was not in this awesome demonstration of power. There was no revelation of God as there might have been on another occasion.

The tornado was followed by an earthquake. Now with the earth moving in convulsion, slicing the valley floor open, yawning for a minute or two and then slamming shut with a shudder, that surely was terrifying enough to be a definite sign that God was present. But no, He was not there, either.

Finally, there was fire. It must have come crashing like lightning and thunder all around the mountain. Surely that would be reminiscent of the events that had just taken place on Mount Carmel, but once again that was not to be.

A NEW SENSE OF GOD'S PRESENCE

It was only in a small voice that Elijah suddenly sensed the presence of God. These three awesome natural phenomena were merely heralds of God's approach. Thus God's word to Elijah, and to us, is simply this: *I am not always to be found in the great and visible movements of the day. I often like to work gently, softly and in a still, small voice.* All too often we who are in God's work wish for the large masses of people to be present and to openly acknowledge the call of the Scriptures upon their lives. We long for the approval of the populace, the palace and the press. But God's way is to present Himself and His gentle word. Accordingly, the first sign of God's goodness is to be found in a new sense of His presence. And His presence would not always be a flamboyant, sensational extravaganza. His presence would often be signaled only by the effectively operating word of God.

Interpreters have once again tried to plow with the heifer from another passage in an attempt to get some deeper truth out of these three signs here. M. B. Van't Veer has collected these conveniently in his study of Elijah.

The first interpretation attempts to see here a major change in prophecy in which God now rejected outward force such as the violence of the tornado, earthquake, and fire. Now He would work by means of the Holy Spirit. The problem with this view is that Elijah was commanded to anoint two men in verses 15-17 who would still wreak havoc through outward force. Moreover, God also would yet call down fire and consume two belligerent army captains.

A more common interpretation is to make the first three signs into a representation of the law and to reserve the small voice as a representation of the gospel. But this division pits God against Himself, for He reveals Himself in law as well as gospel. Nor is the Old Testament the only place where the fury of His judgments may be seen. The fact is that each of these signs had been used as avenues of theophany and continued to be used as such into the later periods of history.

Parallel to this view is one that attempts to make a change in the whole prophetic mission by rebuking, as it were, that type of prophecy that is connected with human passion and zeal in favor of a prophecy that highlights the mercy and graciousness of God. But this too forces an unnatural division into the Godhead, supposing that mercy and love are more authentic characteristics and that justice and wrath are totally out of keeping with a proper view of God. Moreover, the subsequent prophets and apostles exhibited from time to time the very characteristics which this view champions as being now defunct.[1]

A NEW SENSE OF GOD'S LOVE

The only proper view that meets all the facts in this text is that God is giving His servant a bigger view of Himself than the prophet could recall in the midst of his disappointment and disillusionment. If God were patient with Israel for all those years in the wilderness, and if He were patient with His servant during Elijah's forty days of bitter meandering in that same desert, would He not be able to mix the proper amount of justice with love when the appropriate time came?

There would not be a fiery display as an encore to the Mount Carmel incident. Elijah needed a reminder that God is also a God of love, grace and mercy. His reason for so regarding Israel (and Elijah!) is His covenant and the promise He had made long ago. As 2 Kings 13:23 reminds us, "The LORD was gracious to them and had respect for them because of his covenant with Abraham, Isaac, and Jacob and would not destroy them, neither cast He them from His presence *as yet*" (italics mine).

A FRESH CALL TO SERVICE

But God was not finished with His servant as yet either, for Elijah would now enter into some of his most productive years. God would now apply His final cure for all Elijah's blues about himself and the work to which he had been called: He would issue Elijah a fresh call to service and restore him to a new sphere of usefulness (verses 15-21).

God commissioned Elijah to anoint two kings and a companion/successor to the prophetic mission which he had inaugurated. Moreover, in this same period of time Elijah would leave a mark on the theological horizon that would rarely be achieved in the history of Israel: He would found three or four theological schools for the training of members of the prophetic group. These seminaries would each grow to approximately fifty students each by the time of his death.

This turned out to be the most productive period of Elijah's life, even though we are not given a day-by-day journal of all that happened. This is only natural since the Bible is a story about God and His works, not about the works of men.

So the Lord gave to Elijah a fresh call to serve Him even as He gave a similar call to the disciple Peter after his terrible denial of his Lord. When Peter had recovered from his debacle, God's word to him was "Feed my sheep" (John 21:16). Likewise, Elijah was given a whole new set of orders.

He would be the new king-maker, for he was to anoint the king over the neighboring nation of Syria: the usurper Hazael. He would also anoint the overly ambitious army captain named Jehu, the son of Nimshi, as king over Israel. The tasks these men would accomplish would be bound up with the kingdom of God, for all who survived and escaped the scourge

of the military advances made by Hazael would be picked up
in the lethal blows delivered by Jehu.

Indeed, that is what happened to a reluctant and unrepen-
tant Israel which continued to flaunt the grace and message of
Yahweh: King Jehoram survived the battle against Hazael (2
Kings 8:29), but he was put to death later by Jehu (2 Kings
9:24). Hazael also chastised Israel in raid after raid, but Jehu
was God's further instrument of judgment, not only in seeing
that Jezebel met a most violent death (2 Kings 9:33), but that
all the new priests and prophets of Baal once again were
slaughtered (2 Kings 10:25). All of this was predicted by the
Lord in 1 Kings 19:17 along with the pointed remark that there
were seven thousand other individuals in Israel who had not
bowed their knees to Baal (1 Kings 19:18).

THE CALL OF ELISHA

The text takes more space to describe the call of Elisha.
Elijah encountered him while Elisha was busy working on his
father's farm. This was not one of the poorer farms in Israel,
for Elisha's father was operating twelve tractors — twelve yoke
of oxen. The young man Elisha was working with the twelfth
pair when Elijah approached him in the field, threw his mantle
over him and kept on going. All in Israel knew this mantle
as the sign of the prophetic office just as we today can tell
most people's professions or walks of life by some of the
distinctive clothes associated with their jobs.

When Elisha realized what Elijah had done, he dropped
everything and ran to follow his new master. There was never
a moment's hesitation: His dedication to the call was decisive
and total. His only request was to return and bid good-bye to
his friends and family. Elijah was more than happy to agree
to this request.

The gladness and enthusiasm of Elisha's dedication must
have been another welcomed indication to Elijah that God
indeed was ready to favor him and use him once again. The
young intern was so thrilled over being called into God's high
service, leaving a wealthy and prosperous background enjoyed
by probably very few in Israel, that he decided to throw a
party. Right then and there he slaughtered his yoke of oxen
and prepared a banquet. What his father thought of seeing his
"tractor" being butchered and having his son walk off the farm

for some unexplained calling of the Lord, we do not know. But one thing for sure: Such a high calling into God's service was not a time for moaning and sadness, but of rich banqueting and rejoicing.

If only this mentality would return to our circles again today! We tend to spare only those who probably will not have a rich career in business, thinking that the Lord can use any and all "weak" vessels. In Elisha's day, the mentality was the reverse. When God called someone, it was a most fantastic event. It should rival a wedding in its festive aspects, and so it did.

Several years ago I was preaching on this text just outside of Tokyo, Japan. One of my former students was translating for me into Japanese and doing a marvelous job when we came upon this section of the text. I made the observations I have just noted here, telling about the wonderful joy with which this event was received and how they all entered into it with a sumptuous feast.

At this point my interpreter's translation of my English comments suddenly lengthened and he went on and on while I waited. Then I heard him say one Japanese word I had recently learned: *sukiyaki*. Now I knew I had not mentioned anything about that, so I looked at him in front of that audience of about four hundred men and women with puzzlement. Then I realized what he had done. It had been explained to me that sukiyaki was a meal originally prepared by Japanese farmers out in their fields — they used their plows as a cooking utensil and made a most delicious meal. The Japanese loved this allusion — to think that the Old Testament tells of a sukiyaki meal. They nodded in delight and approval while I regained my sense of location in my message. My translator later apologized for doing exactly what I would have done to contemporize the word of God to their situation if I had known their culture better. Our joy that afternoon was as delightful as the joy of Elisha's house that one of their finest men had heard the call of God and was willing to respond.

FOCUS ON GOD'S FAITHFULNESS

What then can we say to discouraged men and women? Does God have any concern and effective cures for those who go through severe times of depression? This text shouts a loud

"Yes!" This is not to say that physical or medical help may not be needed; indeed it may be. But why do we so often feel that there is no help for such miseries within the church?

The faithfulness of God is the reminder that is needed here. Said the apostle Paul, "No temptation has overtaken you, but such as is common to man, *but God is faithful,* who will not let you be tempted above that which you are able to bear, but He will with the temptation make a way of escape that you may be able to bear it" (1 Corinthians 10:13). And again, "If we believe not, *yet He abideth faithful:* He cannot deny Himself" (2 Timothy 2:13).

The only effective way to turn defeat into determination is to recall once again the faithfulness of the Lord, who promised to be present in our deepest dilemma. We need to recall all the proofs He has given us of His love, and to see all the goodness of His person, character and work. Only then can defeat be turned into a fresh call to service. If you're depressed and discouraged, focus on all the proofs God has given you in the past of His love for you. Reflect on the goodness of His person, character and work. See the living Lord pass before your eyes and be conscious of the fact that you are now standing, praying and serving in His presence.

HOW TO TURN DEFEAT INTO DETERMINATION
1 Kings 19:9-21

1. After Elijah retreated and pouted, what specific things did God do to lift His servant's spirits? Does God minister to us in similar ways today? Give some examples from your own experiences or acquaintances.
2. This segment of Elijah's life shows us how dwelling on the goodness and greatness of God can lift us from defeat to renewal. List at least ten ways in which God has shown His power and faithfulness to you during the past year.
3. When you feel discouraged or "all alone" in the future, focus on God's faithfulness and love. Ask Him to give you a "fresh call to service," then get back into action as Elijah did, trusting God for renewed effectiveness as you minister to others.

7

Where Is God When Unjust Things Happen to Good People?
1 Kings 21

How would you react if you were told the same sad tale that the prophet Nathan told to King David? Do you recall how he wrenched David's heart by describing how a rich aristocrat entertained a traveler by filching from a poor man his only remaining ewe lamb to prepare a meal for his guest, rather than providing for him from his own large herds (2 Samuel 12:4)? It is enough to make one's blood boil. No wonder David "burned with anger against the man" (2 Samuel 12:5).

Injustice, especially at the hands of those in government who are meant to uphold justice, fairness, and equity, is most reprehensible. If you cannot expect to receive a fair hearing and reasonable adjudication of grievances from judges, magistrates, mayors, presidents and kings, then where can you find it here on earth? Government is God's gift to us, to bring as large a measure of justice as possible while we wait for the only fully righteous government of our Lord when He returns again.

Unfortunately, the experience of men and women all too frequently runs against this expectation. Indeed, the mood of the hour can be seen in the large amount of literature on management and leadership which blatantly focuses on subjects such as "power," "aggression," "manipulation," and "intimidation." All too often the object is to put the manager, the company, or the government in the dominant position. It feeds a basic philosophy of selfishness, greed, and personal advancement.

1 Kings 21 is another of those sad episodes in which the government felt it could do whatever it wanted to whomever it wished without being responsible to insure that justice was carried out. The biblical phrase that describes this kind of cavalier brinkmanship is "Sell[ing one's self] to do evil in the eyes of the LORD" (1 Kings 21:20).

TEN YEARS PASS

But we are getting ahead of our story. Let's pick up where we left the prophet Elijah after his experience at Mount Sinai. The Bible does not give many details of his ministry for the next ten years, for it was not God's purpose to give a stenographer's report on each event in the lives of all the main characters. But the new team of Elijah and Elisha had much to do. A. W. Pink conjectures: "It would seem that, following the example of Samuel (1 Samuel 10:5-10,19,20), they established schools here and there fitting young men unto the prophetic office, instructing them in the knowledge of God's law and preparing them to become expounders of it unto the people, and also to lead in psalmody — an important service indeed. We base this view on the mention of 'the sons of the prophets that were at Bethel and at Jericho,' (2 Kings 2:3,5)."[1]

Part of the reason why Elijah and Elisha could devote their full energies to such peaceful activities without royal interference from either the bellicose Jezebel or her puppet husband Ahab was that Ahab was kept occupied most of the time in a desperate struggle with the king of Syria. This is the only event narrated that falls into that ten-year period. It is another incident where the king manifests his ignorance or sheer disregard for the word of God as it was recorded in the law of Moses.

Conceivably, there was some excuse for his wife Jezebel and her ignorance about the law of God: She never pretended to be a follower of Yahweh or of His will. But what can we say in defense of Ahab, who was raised in an environment where the word of God was all too readily available?

The incident involved a man named Naboth, who owned a fine piece of property in the town of Jezreel, bordering on the edge of Ahab's summer palace grounds. Ahab was attracted to this piece of property and politely inquired of Naboth whether he could purchase it. Ostensibly, he wanted to have it in order to plant a vegetable garden.

NABOTH OBEYS GOD'S COMMAND

Now all of this was fair as far as it went, but what the king had forgotten or had put out of his consideration was that this was an impossible request. Scripture clearly forbade the sale of one's property, for the land belonged primarily to the Lord and not to the individuals who lived on it. Leviticus 25:23 taught, "The land shall not be sold forever, for the land is mine, says the LORD." Again in Numbers 36:7 the thought is echoed, "The sons of Israel shall retain the inheritance of the tribe of their fathers." Thus what Ahab was asking for was forbidden by God.

The preservation of one's inheritance was not just a worldly wise act or a shrewd business move; it was not even a sentimental act of keeping the old homestead in the family for generations to honor grandparents or the like. Rather, it was a religious duty closely associated with the promise of the covenant of God. To play fast and loose with the land aspects of the covenant was to start playing fast and loose with the rest of the provisions of that same covenant and the whole plan of God for Israel and the world: One act was only symptomatic of another. Ezekiel 46:18 makes it plain that even the king himself could not force someone off his property.

The ancient tell of Jezreel still stands today, overlooking the plain of Esdraelon (or Meggido plain). I stood on this mound a few years ago. It was overgrown with weeds and littered with the debris of years of occupation on the site. The view was breathtaking and the breezes were cool and refreshing. As I faced north, the town of Meggido was at about the 10 o'clock position. At the 11 o'clock position I could see Mount

Carmel, some eighteen miles away. That was the same route traveled by Elijah in his joyful anticipation of the arrival of rain and God's answer that day by fire. Almost in the same direction, but closer on the horizon, was the town of Nazareth where Jesus grew up and played on high cliffs that rimmed the huge flat plains below. In the middle of this plain was the main highway, which carried all the main traffic flowing through the whole fertile crescent — the merchants, peasants, and armies that moved from Egypt to Syria and beyond over to Mesopotamia.

At the foot of this tell there remains even to this day the clear line of demarkation where the fields of the plain begin. There is no doubt in my mind that this is the very spot Ahab had chosen, but which belonged to the family of Naboth. An orchard of trees now stands where Naboth's vineyard grew in Elijah's time.

The king offered to buy the vineyard outright or to give another piece of vineyard property in exchange for it. But Naboth, out of respect for God and His word, declined both of these offers: "The LORD forbid that I should give you the inheritance of my fathers" (verse 3).

THE CHOICE: OBEY MAN'S LAW OR GOD'S LAW?

There will be times when we as believers will be forced to make a choice between complying with human conventions or complying with the word of God. Some of these choices will be no easier than this one; for after all, this was not the request of just another fellow Israelite. It was the request of Naboth's king!

Daniel's three friends were faced with a similar dilemma when they were told to worship the image set up by the king or be cast into the fiery furnace. Shadrach, Meshach and Abednego just plain refused; their God demanded exclusive worship. He also could deliver them from the fire itself; but if He chose not to deliver them, nothing was changed. They refused to worship any dumb idol (Daniel 3:16,17). There are times when we must say "no" and mean it, for we have been given clear instructions.

Likewise, Peter and John were given orders to cease preaching in public or face imprisonment. Their rejoinder was to politely inform the Sanhedrin that they had no choice: They must preach, for that is what God had commanded them to do (Acts 4:18).

Thus, no government can order a child of God to do anything which Scripture sets forth to the contrary. But if government or any other authority should take a contrary course to the clear teachings of the word of God, then the believer has no choice but to refuse to do what that authority wants him to do and to leave the outcome to God. A. W. Pink wisely commented, "Settle it in your own mind, . . . it is no sin to defy human authorities if they require of you something that manifestly clashes with the law of the Lord. On the other hand, the Christian should be a pattern to others of a law-abiding citizen, so long as God's claims on him [or her] be not infringed."[2]

Naboth's response was that "the Lord forbid" him to accept the king's offer. Therefore, nothing could change what God had spoken — not money, nor political clout, nor intimidation, nor promise of gain, nor the prospect of a better piece of property, nor the prospect of having a special inside track with royalty. He just was not at personal liberty to accept the offer; he was bound by the command of God.

AHAB'S WIMP ROUTINE

With that Ahab became "sullen and angry" (verse 5). This was by now becoming a favorite pattern for this monarch when he was unable to get his own way or when he was displeased with the way things were going. Had he not reacted in exactly the same way when he had been chastised by another unnamed prophet after he released the captured Syrian king, Ben-Hadad (1 Kings 20:43)?

Off he went to sulk in his royal chamber, like a spoiled child refusing to eat. He flopped on his bed and turned his head to the wall and pouted. The picture we are given of the king's moodiness and childishness goes a long way in explaining why Jezebel had been able to take over so much of the reigns of government. How could he even begin to think of ruling a nation when he could not even rule his own emotions?

Enter Jezebel once again — and enter trouble as well. She could not believe that her husband would admit defeat so easily. When would her wimpy husband ever learn what it meant to be a king? What's the use of being a king if you can't use the power of the office for your own ends? She had never seen the likes of this kind of action in the pagan home she grew up in. Back in Sidon, Phoenicia, what her father said as king was what happened. No one would dare cross him. So why wasn't her husband acting like a real king instead of like a spoiled brat and a ninety-seven-pound weakling in need of a Charles Atlas body building course?

Jezebel wanted an explanation for these unprofessional attitudes and actions. Why was the king "sullen?" Why wouldn't he eat?

Ahab's explanation was a master-stroke in the fine art of rationalization. He carefully deleted any and all references to the law of God — a reference that would only have infuriated his wife anyway — and he pretended that it was totally a case of mean obstinacy and unpatriotic insubordination on the part of Naboth. Never mind telling Jezebel about Naboth's conscience or about the fact that Yahweh is Lord of all creation and this was against His law.

Jezebel's scorn for her husband knew no bounds as she sneered, "Is that how you act as a king of Israel?" (verse 7). But never mind, she would handle things as she usually did, especially when they got into a jam. Says Matthew Henry of Jezebel, "Under the pretense of comforting her afflicted husband, she feeds pride and passion, blowing the coals of his own corruption."

JEZEBEL GETS HER WAY AGAIN

Jezebel's diabolical stratagems included the following: forgery of letters from the king; deliberate hypocrisy simulating deep spiritual concern over the fact that they might be under some immediate danger of judgment from God because of some newly revealed evidence of sin in their midst (Jezebel? Concerned about evil and the possible judgment of God? That's a switch!); out and out perjury induced by two sons of Belial; and the orchestrated death of Naboth.

Here was a woman who feared no one, not even Yahweh. She was capable of doing anything in order to win her way. Her plan was to have Naboth done away with on grounds which the same law she despised provided for: blasphemy. Two scoundrels would be hired who would falsely accuse Naboth of cursing both God and the king.

Isn't it amazing how those who reject the word of God will still feel free to use it for their own purposes? That surely was the case here. Deuteronomy 17:6 and 19:15, not to mention Numbers 35:30, required at least two witnesses for any crime that was punishable by death. In order to have the guise of godliness and to win the favor of even the most holy sensibilities, Jezebel made sure she went by "the Book." Moreover, the charge was a serious biblical offense. Exodus 22:27 warned against cursing God and the king while Leviticus 24:14 warned against blaspheming God.

Jezebel sent out notices in the name of the king calling for a national day of fasting. The presumption was that someone had sinned grievously and therefore there had to be a time of fasting until the culprit was found so that the divine sentence against the people could be lifted. The whole situation was a cheap trick and it made a sham out of true religion. Can you imagine the backroom laughter over this one after Jezebel and Ahab had pulled it off? Religion, they would jest, does have its advantages once in a while!

Wickedness almost always exposes itself, for it becomes too self-confident, careless, and intoxicated with its own success. Consequently it makes major blunders which begin to reveal its true nature and purpose. In this case, Jezebel failed to notice that the law of God did not provide for the transfer of a blasphemer's property to the crown; instead, such property was to be forfeited to the Lord as a *herem* (*i.e.*, an involuntary offering of all that existed), the reverse of a voluntary dedication as in the whole burnt offering of Leviticus 1 and Romans 12:1,2. Only the property of traitors was forfeited to the king. Such a selective use of God's word must not happen among believers. That is why believers are urged to read and apply the whole counsel of God — including the Old Testament, lest we too become guilty of another type of selective reading of the text.

NABOTH IS PUT TO DEATH

Thus the day arrived and poor Naboth was singled out for special treatment. The two hired political hacks ceremoniously took their seats opposite Naboth. They both testified that they had heard Naboth curse God and the king. In a flash the people had their answer as to why God allegedly was angry with them; of course, blasphemy was a serious thing. And so Naboth and his family (2 Kings 9:26) were hauled out of the city like common criminals and stoned to death.

Where is justice in all of this? The Bible does not say that Naboth was guilty; in fact, it clearly affirms that they murdered this man and stole his property (verse 19). It is no wonder that this woman Jezebel is remembered as "that woman Jezebel who led my people into immorality and taught them wickedness" (Revelation 2:20). Together with her henchmen, she broke almost every one of the Ten Commandments. She made herself God instead of the Lord (the first commandment). She took the name of the Lord in vain as she made her goons swear in the name of God that they had heard what they did not (the third commandment). Incidentally, they did not use the covenantal name of Yahweh which implied a relationship to Him, but the more indefinite name Elohim. She was also a murderer (the sixth commandment). She stole another man's land (the eighth). She and the two scoundrels gave false testimony (the ninth) and Ahab coveted what were his neighbor's belongings (the tenth). In this one incident, they violated six of the Ten Commandments.

Right is not always immediately avenged, nor is wrong continually frustrated and hampered. In our present evil age, all too often wickedness has its day and righteousness appears to take a terrific beating. Why does God allow such unmitigated injustice to press its case? Could He not have thundered from heaven, as He did at Mount Carmel, and consume these liars in a moment? That would have taught Jezebel a good lesson.

THE PROBLEM OF EVIL

The problem of evil is not a simple issue. It is probably more complex than any other single issue in the whole of Christian theology. In 1981, Rabbi Harold S. Kushner wrote his bestseller entitled, *When Bad Things Happen to Good People*. Life forced him to grapple with this question of the presence of evil when he was told one day by the doctors that his three-year-old son Aaron had progeria and that he would not live to reach his teens. Immediately the old question came crashing in on Kushner's consciousness: "Why do people who don't deserve the things they suffer still face such misfortune?" Which aspect of the divine nature is unable to operate in such a circumstance? Is it God's goodness or His power?

Rabbi Kushner finally decided to locate the problem in God's power, for he had to believe that God was all good and that He wanted to help those in distress; He indeed was doing everything He could, but He did not have unlimited power. Therefore, Kushner had to conclude that God was not omnipotent![3]

We cannot agree with this answer, for it, too, violates part of the biblical picture. God is both totally good and all-powerful. Anything less than this would not be the God of the Scriptures. Christians are not frightened by the presence of evil. They understand that it came about as a result of man's sin in the Garden of Eden. In fact, the whole message of the gospel is to meet the presence of evil head on. The presence of evil is all too real; Christians cannot pretend that it does not exist. It does and it is wrong and it must go.

Neither do Christians have the slightest doubt as to how this is all going to come out. That is already a foregone conclusion now that we have witnessed the resurrection of Jesus Christ from the dead. He holds the power over death and evil; they are already doomed.

The issue, however, that believers struggle with most is the *origin* of evil, not its presence or its outcome. Why did God ever allow evil to get a toehold in the first place? Now there is the $64,000 question. The answer, of course, involves the desire of God to have men and women love him freely; therefore, freedom must enter into the discussion. If individuals are to choose freely what they do or do not do, the risk will always be present that some will make the wrong moral choice. In this case, Jezebel and her two stooges did just that.

What about those who are crushed in the meantime and who cry out to God for relief? Can't He hear them cry, "How long, O Lord?" Would it not have been better to have many more prophets of Yahweh ready for service after the rains came? Why then did God allow (and that is the proper word, for God is not the direct sponsor or author of evil) Jezebel to be successful in her purge?

WHEN CHRISTIANS HURT

The question is similar to the one that the church asks when fellow Christians are martyred or taken in untimely death, or endure intense hardship, suffering or injustice.

But there are no easy answers here, for we're attempting to probe the mind of God. Who among us can say that we have served as God's counselor? Or that we know better than He does what foolishness to put up with and which evil to halt? The topic has an element of mystery to it, for it involves the deepest questions about the character of God. We can be sure that our Lord had both the power and the goodness necessary to do what needed to be done. Yet, for the moment, He let evil have its day in the sun — perhaps in order to extend His mercy and longsuffering even more to the likes of a Jezebel so that neither she nor anyone else could ever complain that they were programmed to play out the role of antagonist so that God might be glorified in the end. There is no way any could say that — least of all Ahab and Jezebel. They both sowed sin and evil with both hands, yet a loving Lord continued to wait patiently for each to come to their senses.

God is angry with the wicked every day, yet He loves the sinner while He simultaneously hates their sin. C. S. Lewis said this theological aphorism used to make him uncomfortable because he judged that God either loved him or He did not. *How could God hate what I did as a sinner without hating me?* he asked. But then it dawned on Lewis that this was not so hard, since that was exactly what he had done with himself. He certainly disliked some of the things he did, but he did not thereby reject his own self. *So why couldn't God do the same thing?* he asked. The problem evaporated.

After Naboth's murder, Elijah entered the picture. It began, as usual, with a command from God to go meet Ahab. Certainly the cry of Naboth's innocent blood came up before the throne of God and pleaded for vindication. Just as Ahab "went down to take possession of Naboth's vineyard" (verse 16), God's word swung into action against this thief. Ahab could not beg off and blame his wife for all that had happened. His complicity was total. Moreover, he was held as being more responsible since he was charged before God as the head of the kingdom and he was the one who grew up in Israel and had been exposed to the word.

When Elijah and Ahab met, Ahab scoffed, "So you have found me, my enemy?" (verse 20). How's that for a greeting to one of God's servants and one who had been extremely gracious to this hardened potentate? Had not Ahab seen the mighty works that God had done at the hands of Elijah? What does it take for some people to repent? What more evidence could Ahab want? His enemy was not Elijah; on the contrary, Ahab felt himself an enemy of God!

Ahab was the one to be pitied, not Elijah. The king was actually in bondage to sin and to himself. He needed deliverance more than did poor, murdered Naboth. Naboth's condition was temporary, but Ahab and Jezebel's would be permanent if they did not start paying attention to the gracious work and word of God.

AHAB REPENTS, AND GOD SHOWS MERCY

Thus when Elijah let the full weight of the message of God's judgment fall on Ahab, the king was suddenly sobered as never before. He immediately donned the clothes of a penitent and sat in sackcloth (verse 27). And well he should, for the writer observes in an aside: "There never was a man like Ahab who sold himself to do evil in the eyes of the LORD, urged on by Jezebel his wife. He behaved in the vilest manner by going after idols, like the Ammorites the LORD drove out before Israel" (verse 25). In other words, Ahab took the prize for being the most wicked person in Israel and Jezebel came in second as the chief instigator and agitator for evil.

The judgment of God on their lives read this way: Ahab and all his male descendants would be cut off from this life. Furthermore, his kingdom and dynasty would come to an abrupt end. God's reason is stated in verse 22: "Because you have provoked me to anger and caused Israel to sin."

Elijah also had a word for Jezebel: The dogs would devour her by the wall of Jezreel (verse 23). In fact the dogs would eat all of Ahab's family who died in the city and the birds of the air would feast on all of his family who died in the open fields (verse 24). The slow-moving wheels of justice had turned, and they had ground everything ever so fine. Justice would finally have her day in court.

Verse 27 surprises us with an unexpected reversal: "When Ahab heard these words, he tore his clothes, put on sackcloth and fasted. He lay in sackcloth and went around meekly." It almost seems contrived — Ahab fasting and taking a meek stance in life?

But the grace of God was still operating, for Elijah was given one more word from God. He was asked if he had noticed how humble and contrite Ahab had become since hearing these solemn words of judgment. Since Ahab had responded, even at this late hour, God would not bring the disaster in his day, but would delay it until the days of his son.

CONDITIONAL PROPHECY: GOD'S JUSTICE AND GOD'S MERCY

This introduces the subject of conditional prophecy. Most prophecy is conditional, with an unexpressed "unless you repent" message (except that which is connected with the inviolable oath of God such as the promise He made with the seasons in Noah's day; His covenant with Abraham, Isaac and Jacob; His covenant with David; the New Covenant; and the promise of the New Heavens and the New Earth).

The theology of conditional prophecy is set forth in Jeremiah 18:7-10. There the prophet notes the alternative prospect for fulfillment of either the divine words of judgment or the divine blessing. The end results depend on the response of those to whom the prophecies are spoken, for even though the words sound as if they allow no exception and the judgment is certain, the consequences will only be carried out as pronounced if the individual fails to respond to the invitation of God to repent. Likewise, for those who are blessed and who have enjoyed the prophetic pronouncement of success and prosperity, their fortunes can be suddenly reversed if they presume on their walk with God.

Jeremiah 18:7-10 is an extremely important passage if we are to handle such statements as Elijah gives in his prophecy. God does not change in His being, acting, or word; only men change. That is what will affect all the words the prophets speak, for they are conditioned on what happens in the hearts and lives of the listeners.

When Ahab repented, God mercifully cancelled the heavy load of explicit judgment against him. That is why the message of the prophets is still relevant for us today, for the blessings and judgments of God upon us, either on an individual or corporate basis, have a conditional and alternative prospect. It is not purely an academic matter as to how we will respond to these words.

WHAT GOES AROUND, COMES AROUND

Even if the repentance of Ahab may have been only momentary and purely external, God still gave him His promise so long as Ahab followed Him. However, when Ahab went back on his word and again lapsed into all his evil ways, he was cut down in battle by a random shot of an archer who drew his bow without aiming at anything in particular and it wounded the proud Ahab. Indeed, the dogs did lick up his blood as Ahab's chariot returned to the city with the stains of his life-blood all over it (1 Kings 22:38). Thus he suffered an ignominious and disgraceful death which he easily could have avoided had he listened to the repeated warnings of God's servants.

Jezebel suffered every bit as gruesome a death. As prophesied, she was tossed from a palace window, trampled by the hooves of Jehu's horses, and left for dogs to devour (2 Kings 9:30-37).

Ahab's son Joram had his corpse cast into the field of Naboth's vineyard (2 Kings 9:25,26); thus, justice was finally served.

The point is that Elijah was not a false prophet, for he "had stood in [God's] counsel, and had caused [God's] people to hear [God's] words" (Jeremiah 23:22). The problem was that the king, his queen and the nation were slow to turn from their wicked ways and from their evil doings. Ahab should have ripped his heart, as the prophet Joel advised in another connection, rather than merely ripping his garments (Joel 2:13).

It grieves our Lord when we and our generation are willing to disregard His laws and His character as our only perfect norm for deciding what is ethical and what is right. Instead, too many of us have become a law unto ourselves and have accepted the mores and standards of the day.

How can we view the national phenomenon of nearly eighteen million abortions in the past decade or so and wonder how long it will be before the judgment of God strikes us? Will our Lord let us as a nation get off free, when He judged Germany for sending six million Jews to their deaths? We have tripled that record by consigning little human beings to garbage dumpsters.

And what shall we say about a whole host of social and

personal ills that have surfaced in our nation? Do these not cry out for as much justice as did the unnecessary death of Naboth and his family? We must refuse to be sold into the bondage of doing evil, for the one that is born of God does not practice sin (1 John 3:6,9).

God knew of Naboth's unfair treatment, for even though He did not think it best to deliver Naboth out of the hands of his false accusers, He did not let the matter slide. God does keep exceedingly fine books. There *is* a payday. For wily Jezebel and reckless Ahab, it came with suddenness and finality.

WHEN UNJUST THINGS HAPPEN TO GOOD PEOPLE

1 Kings 21

1. From your perspective, what are some of the reasons God allows bad things to happen to His people? Think of a bad or unfair incident in your life: In what ways do you feel God has used (or will use) the incident for good?

2. Name at least three areas where tension might arise (as it did for Naboth) between the call of Scripture and the demands of government. If such a tension becomes a reality in your life, how will you deal with it? What will be your scriptural basis?

3. Most prophecies to errant nations are conditional — God will not bring judgment if He sees repentance. Likewise, most prophecies of peace and prosperity are conditional upon the recipient's staying true to God. Think of at least two real-life examples (historical or contemporary) of each of these two types of prophecies. What conclusions can you draw regarding the future of our nation?

8

Who's In Charge Here?
1 Kings 22 — 2 Kings 1:6

Whenever something starts to go wrong at the shop, office or school, the first question that top management wants answered by middle managers is, "Who's in charge here?" Someone has to be responsible for what does or does not happen.

But to whom shall we direct that same question when things start to fall apart on a national level? Especially when the trouble seems to be beyond all human means of prevention? For example, when a storm wipes out your newly built navy before it can even sail out of dry-dock, who's in charge of that? When calamity befalls even the royal household, who's in charge of that? When 102 admittedly insolent soldiers are suddenly struck down by fire from heaven, who's in charge of that? And when a prophet is removed from his term of service by a chariot of fire and the man who had played second fiddle for so long is suddenly left with the total responsibility resting on his shoulders, it's time once again to ask, "Who's in charge here?"

The biblical text asked this same question, only it was not as uncommitted as we are in our modern expression. We presume that the final court of appeal and the ultimate area of responsibility are to be found in some human being. It rarely strikes the thought of modern men and women that that question might best be asked on a much broader scale. 2 Kings 1 does not share our modern embarrassment or hesitancies: It wades right into the middle of the fray and asks with more than a little bit of implied rebuke, "Is it because there is no God in Israel that you are going to consult with Baal-Zebub, the god of Ekron?" (verses 3,6,16).

Three times the question is thrown down as a gauntlet. Did Israel (and do we today) think that God is dead and that there are no other dimensions to life than those which appear to us on the surface?

Of course, we would want to respond in self-defense by focusing on the shameful fact that in Israel's case, an idol was being consulted. Our defense would take this shape: "Who would be stupid enough to go ask a dumb image of wood or stone a question that only intelligent, living beings ought to answer? Idolatry is not our cup of tea."

WHY DO WE ACT AS IF THERE IS NO GOD?

Two responses must be made to this disclaimer. First, idolatry *is* one of our problems, for any time we make any person, committee, institution, job, hobby, idea, or goal number one in our lives, we are head-long into full-blown idolatry. The genius of idolatry is the act of putting anything or any person or idea in number one position ahead of the living God. Therefore the matter of whether it involves attaching loyalty to a hunk of inert stone is not germane to the heart of this argument.

But even more fundamentally we must ask: *Why do we act as if there is no God?* The issue is one of *practical* atheism! Too frequently the only causes we attribute to most events are those which are secondary and visible. We say it was an unusual storm, or the luck of the draw. It is almost anything except God Himself. But the question will not go away: *Is God in the land, or isn't He?*

Four magnificent episodes demonstrate that God indeed was resident in the land and indeed was in charge. They begin at the end of 1 Kings (22:41) and continue through 2 Kings 2:15. These events record:

1. the destruction of the jointly sponsored navy of Ahaziah (Ahab's son) and Jehoshaphat (King of Judah)
2. Ahaziah's fall through the lattice and his inquiry about his medical prognosis
3. the three companies of fifty men sent out to haul Elijah before the brazen King Ahaziah
4. Elijah's translation to heaven in the chariot of fire drawn by horses of fire.

We will examine the first two episodes in this chapter.

GOD IS IN CHARGE OF NATURE

The first event teaches us that God is in charge of nature. It is of no use blaming the weatherman for things that even mystify these not-often-befuddled men of science. And whom shall we say Ahaziah and Jehoshaphat had to blame in their day when weathermen had not yet appeared on the scene?

All was not lost, however. Jehoshaphat was spared even greater losses when he had this initial minor damage inflicted on his government. It happened this way. The king of Judah, always a man who sought conciliation and cooperation wherever he could, once again had been drawn into an alliance with the wicked son of Ahab, Ahaziah, which he should never have considered in the first place.

Jehoshaphat was so different from the northern king Ahaziah that one wonders if he were not just a bit naive. But the Scripture is clear on the fact that Jehoshaphat truly loved the Lord and wanted to serve Him. "In everything he walked in the ways of his father Asa and did not stray from them; he did what was right in the eyes of the LORD" (1 Kings 22:43). Already we had been told in 1 Kings 15:14 that "The heart of Asa was wholly true to the LORD all his days." Thus, in this case the influence of the lives of his parents had had a great impact on Jehoshaphat. While it is true that he did leave some of the high places and altars standing (presumably for the worship of Yahweh), nevertheless he did remove all the altars to Baal and Astarte in his southern kingdom of Judah (1 Chronicles 17:6). He also exterminated the cult of the male prostitutes (sodomites) from the land (1 Kings 22:46; c.f. 1

Kings 14:24; 15:12).

GOD REWARDS OBEDIENCE

As a result, the nation was blessed in unusual ways and experienced a time of peace and general prosperity. The truth of this connection between righteousness and the good hand of God upon a people is stated in Proverbs 16:7: "When a man's ways please the LORD, he makes even his enemies to be at peace with him." It is a fact: The prosperity or adversity of a nation is directly related to the attitudes and conduct that the righteous remnant or moral minority has towards God. This is not to say that there are no exceptions to this generality. The exceptions, however, are in themselves usually only temporary interruptions of what is an otherwise unbroken rule of God's moral operation in His universe.

Happy is the nation that has moral and righteous leaders, for these heads of state also set the level of expectation that goodness, justice and right will prevail. And when that which is moral, just and righteous prevails, wickedness is not tolerated nor are its sponsors given free hand to ply their trade.

But it is not just the responsibility of the leaders to see that the will of God is done in their realm; the believing body has just as significant a role to play. When their ways please the Lord, He in turn gives favor to that people and esteem from all who view their nation from the countries around them. Let error, sin, and wickedness creep into the believing body and one may as well write *Ichabod* over all the work of their hands, whether it be their homes, their businesses, their churches, or their nation.

The principle is so clear in Scripture that it is embarrassing to even suggest that this might not be so or that this is too rigid a position. The consequences of flaunting this clear teaching have been played out for all to view over and over again in history with such results as violent social revolution, economic disgrace, natural disasters of gigantic proportions, and the brutality of barbarous border feuds or even of international war.

Jehoshaphat did have one soft spot, however. Too often he had tried to be as friendly as he could with his idolatrous neighbor to the north. He had almost gotten himself killed as an ally to Ahab when they went up to fight together against Ramoth-Gilead (1 Kings 22:32). Undaunted by his previous compromise, he had apparently agreed to join Ahab's son Ahaziah, who was now reigning in Ahab's stead, in constructing and operating a merchant fleet. Jehoshaphat had been warned that this was not what he should be doing as a believer. Graciously God had sent a prophet named Jehu, the son of Hanani, to caution him against this venture: "Should you help the wicked and love those who hate the LORD?" (2 Chronicles 19:2). The divine estimate of Ahaziah's belief is clear — he was one who "hate[d] the LORD."

Jehu continued his warning to Jehoshaphat: "Because of this, the wrath of God is upon you. There is, however, some good in you, for you rid the land of the Asherah poles and set your heart on seeking the LORD" (1 Chronicles 18:2,3). As a result, 1 Kings 22:48 notes that the ships "were wrecked at Ezion Geber," that is, in their port on the Gulf of Aqaba even before they had a chance to set sail.

JEHOSHAPHAT'S UNEQUAL YOKE

If we have any doubts as to who was in charge here and why this event took place, God sent another prophet to Jehoshaphat named Eliezer, son of Dodavahu from Mareshah, who made it perfectly clear that it was not a hurricane or a strong wind that had put these two shipping magnates out of business; it was the Lord Himself. The Lord was in charge.

Explained Eliezer, "Because you have made an alliance with Ahaziah, the LORD will destroy what you have made" (1 Chronicles 20:37). Thus the ships were wrecked and were not able to set sail to trade with the fabled land of Ophir, from which Solomon had derived so many exotic products.

God used the winds and the waves as His messengers to remind His king Jehoshaphat that spiritual compromise is not pleasing to a Lord who will brook no rival. This is the same truth we are taught in 2 Corinthians 6:14-18. It asks, "How can believers be yoked with unbelievers?" Too frequently these verses are interpreted as referring only to disallowing mixed marriages between believers and unbelievers, but the truth has a much broader application. It reaches into every area of life where I might compromise my stand as a believer in order to share a venture of any sort with another person, company, or institution. This is not to say that there are no legitimate relationships into which one may enter with unbelievers. Instead, it is a warning that none of these relationships must take equal stance or superior priority over my relationship with my Lord. Otherwise, I will be back into idolatry once again and I had better have the courage to name it for what it is right from the beginning. As the apostle Paul put it, "What harmony (or concord) is there between Christ and Belial?" (1 Corinthians 6:15). Answer: None!

Jehoshaphat at least demonstrated that he learned well and that he did not rebel against the loving judgment of God on his shipping venture, for when Ahaziah came back a second time and invited him to rebuild what had been destroyed, he firmly declined (1 Kings 22:49). That is the mark of a spiritual person. We may misread the situation once and we may fail to properly apply the teaching of God's Word to a particular issue of life; but when God speaks through the events of life, it is best that we recoup as quickly as possible and obey what we missed the first time around. That is exactly what Jehoshaphat did: he realized who was in charge and he acted accordingly.

Ahaziah did not learn as quickly; in fact he did not learn at all. One would think that after three and a half years of drought and the expose of the total ineffectiveness of Baalism that this son of Ahab would be one smart cookie. Alas, "He did evil in the sight of the LORD, because he walked in the ways of his father and mother . . . He served and worshipped Baal and provoked the LORD, the God of Israel, to anger, just as his father had done" (1 Kings 22:52,53).

AHAZIAH FAILS TO LEARN FROM HISTORY

What a waste! What he learned from history was that nothing was to be learned from it at all. And if fire from heaven did not convince his father and mother to change (he too must have witnessed that event or at least been old enough to remember all the excitement it generated), what would? Some people are so bent on racing down the path to destruction that nothing will slow them down or stop them.

It just did not occur to Ahaziah that God was in charge. He exhibited utter contempt for the past. But God does hold people responsible for the lessons of the past; history is more than the dull repetition of facts and dates that no one is interested in any longer. History, rather, is the stage on which God is acting out His own story for which He holds individuals accountable. When we fail to remember that sin will boomerang on us and bring us reproach, then we must learn by sad experience what others also learned by hard experience.

The king also held the law of God in contempt. Foremost among Ahaziah's failings were his transgressions of the first commandment. Exodus 20:3 had warned that he (and we) should have "no other gods before [the Lord God]." That was merely the beginning of his transgressions, for he would go on to consult wizards and soothsayers in his attempt to get some word from outside himself; a clear violation of the Mosaic word from God (Leviticus 19:31; 20:6,27; Deuteronomy 18:10,11).

Ahaziah's sowing of wild oats began to lead to trouble even though he was in office for a mere two years. Before anyone could act, Moab rebelled against Israel. Moab had been subject to Israel ever since the days of King David. This had netted a lucrative annual tax of 100,000 lamb fleeces and 100,000 ram skins. Suddenly that came to an abrupt halt — which must have had a major effect on the Israelite economy. The resultant upset in the balance of power cost Israel dearly.

HISTORY REPEATS ITSELF: WHEN WILL WE LEARN?

This was not the last time this type of upset would be played out in history, for one need only consider what has happened in recent years in the breakup of the British empire. Could this be purely accidental, and unrelated to the poor state of spiritual affairs in that nation where the preaching of the gospel once moved masses to respond to the Word of God? Currently the situation is the reverse of what it used to be, for all statistics on church attendance, missionary recruits, or financial support for the work of Christ reflect only a modicum of the percentage they once represented in that great nation.

Likewise, the loss of prestige for America overseas and around the world coincided with a period of spiritual struggle in the church during the 1960s. These are not freakish or purely accidental associations of facts: Scripture urges us to relate them directly to each other and then to repent and to urge our brethren to become our nation's keepers. We can mark it down that when God is provoked with churches, politicians, theologians or nations, as He was with Ahaziah, we will also see a corresponding dissolution of the spheres of influence and a lack of success in the endeavors or ventures of the groups that each of these represent.

Whether it was in agitation over Moab's revolt or carelessness in his drunken stupor, Ahaziah fell through the lattice work of an upper story in the palace and severely injured himself. The fall itself could have been immediately fatal, but God graciously gave this rebellious king yet one more final message of His love. There was still time if Ahaziah would humble himself before God. There would be "space for repentance" in order to let him "consider his ways," says A. W. Pink, but instead of responding in repentance and contrition for his sins, he sent to the god of Ekron, Baal-Zebub — "Baal of the flies." More than any other indicator, this act was proof that "his soul was in worse state than his body."[1]

Probably the real name for this Philistine deity was Baal-Zebul — "Baal Prince" or "Lord Prince," which the biblical writer promptly stigmatized as "lord of the flies" since the two words were very similar in Hebrew. Baal could "buzz off" for all Elijah cared.

HAS GOD DIED?

Why would anyone who was raised in Israel and who knew of the great works of God send his messengers to get some wizard or soothsayer connected with Baal-Zebub's operation in the Philistine city of Ekron to render a verdict on his health? Had the God of Israel died? Had He been unfaithful to Israel in the past? Had He failed to show His power in the contemporary world of that day?

To head off this treacherous delegation on what had to be one of the most humiliating undertakings in Israel's history, the Angel of the Lord (a Christophony) Himself instructed Elijah to intercept these messengers and to send them back home with the word they were seeking from demonic sources. Ahaziah would not recover; he would die on his sickbed.

How omniscient is our God! He knew exactly what Ahaziah was saying and doing and He knew where the messengers would be. No wonder Psalm 139:1-6 celebrates this all-knowing characteristic of our Lord. We are totally known by our Lord; nothing escapes His notice or attention.

So powerful was that word on the consciences of these untutored messengers that, even though they had no idea who it was that had intercepted them, they returned to the palace and thereby risked extreme punishment for failing to carry out the king's orders. God above was the only one who could reveal to His servants the prophets His secrets and tell them what would be the outcome of events now taking place.

WHO'S IN CHARGE HERE?

1 Kings 22 — 2 Kings 1:6

1. To what extent do you think God is in control of such things as weather? Is it proper to make a distinction between the directive and the permissive will of God or is this distinction artificial and without any real biblical warrant?
2. Since none of us are prophets in the sense that we receive revelations like those in the Bible, how can we be held responsible for the lessons of history? Refer to Amos 4:6-12 and recall the scenario of events in the United States from 1963 to 1970. What should be your personal responsibility in assuring the future of your nation?
3. How would you define the essence of idolatry and how does it manifest itself today? Could something which is good in and of itself become an idol to keep us away from God? Give at least three examples.

9

The Chariot of Fire
2 Kings 1:6 — 2:13

Elijah was back to his former role. There was none of the previous fear for his life, for the old boldness and courage were once again in evidence. This ought to be a lesson to each of us when we are tempted to pull punches in the pulpit, classroom, Bible study, or witnessing opportunities. Such catering to our audience shows that we fear our audiences more than we fear God.

It did not take Ahaziah very long to figure out who had delivered the dreaded word that he, the king, would die. It was "a man with a garment of hair and a leather belt around his waist" (2 Kings 1:7), explained the messengers, in reply to the king's inquiry about who had known their mission and the correct answer. For most people, that in itself would have been impressive and adequate grounds for trusting the Lord. But not for this hardened sinner. Ahaziah's response was that Elijah was to be brought to his side at once.

Thus far we have seen that God is in charge of the natural

world along with the secrets of life including one's health and the accidents that befall them. This does not mean that He is the author of evil or that He sponsors evil. But He *allows* it — nothing happens without His permission, direction, or possible intervention.

GOING AFTER THE MESSENGER

Angered by the *message* he had heard, Ahaziah decided to go after the *man* who had given it. He would carry out what his mother Jezebel had only threatened. Would this put the prophet to flight, as it had once before? A squadron of fifty soldiers was immediately detailed to roust Elijah from the mountain area which must have been known to be his favorite haunt.

In haughty and dictatorial tones, the army captain ordered Elijah, "Man of God, get down!" There can be little doubt that the designation "man of God" was uttered with a scornful sneer.

Elijah's response was exactly what it should have been years ago to the bitter Jezebel: "If I am a man of God [as you unwittingly testify to], may fire come down from heaven and consume you and your fifty men" (2 Kings 1:10).

Elijah must have indeed been a "man of God," for fire fell from heaven and the fifty-one men were gone. The point is not that God's servant was old and crotchety, slightly short on patience. To insult God's ambassador was to take on God Himself; for what His ambassador said, He said.

Nor is the point that this is another example of the barbarity of Old Testament times, for had this judgment been inappropriate for the gospel era, much less the Old Testament, God would never have answered Elijah's request. The fire was from God, not from any magic that Elijah possessed. Our Lord would never be a part of a spirit of revenge or vindictiveness. This is no more vengeful than the New Testament text which says, "The Lord Jesus shall be revealed from heaven with his mighty angels, in flaming fire taking vengeance on those that know not God and that obey not the gospel of our Lord Jesus Christ" (2 Thessalonians 1:7,8).

It is no wonder that some have difficulty with the doctrine of the eternal judgment on the wicked; they probably began their trouble by rejecting God's right to finally judge those in the Old Testament who continually and finally refused the gracious offer of God.

God responded to Elijah's call to show him His power and to authenticate the fact that He had sent him, not to placate him or to gratify Elijah's sense of pride. Even in the New Testament we are warned against mocking any of that which pertains to the worship of God, for in the same measure as we have trifled with any of those matters, God will trifle with us (1 Corinthians 3:15,16; contrast this with 1 Corinthians 6:19,20).

FIFTY-ONE MORE BITE THE DUST

The second detachment of men and its officer were no less insolent; in fact, this man added the word "at once" or "quickly" to the same haughty order the recently deceased commander had given. Surely the smell of burnt flesh in the air would have alerted and moderated the impudence of this officer, but it was all in vain. He, too, perished along with his fifty men.

The third captain had more sense. His tone was one of entreaty. Moreover, he attributed the source of the fire to its real origins. For him, "fire [had] fallen from heaven" (verse 14); that is to say, it had come from God. Jews of that day were careful not to say God's name for fear of taking it in vain, therefore they usually used some such circumlocution as "heaven" to replace "God" as in the phrase "kingdom of heaven."

To all who show the slightest movement toward acknowledging the presence and power of the word of God, the Angel of the Lord (the Lord Jesus Himself in His pre-incarnate form) waits to grant mercy. In verse 15, we read that He granted such mercy to the third captain.

. . . AND SO DOES AHAZIAH

Elijah went with this humbled officer to visit King Ahaziah's sickbed. Boldly, Elijah repeated his question of rebuke along with his sad prognosis of the king's condition. Enraged as he may have been, the king was in no condition to roar like a lion. Already he had lost 102 men with the same sudden heaven's fire that had appeared years ago in his father's day on Mount Carmel. Then, it had been a fire of sacrifice for the nation's sin, and it had announced that reconciliation was now possible and the blessings of rain were now available. Why did things have to turn this way? Wasn't he the king? Wasn't he in charge here? Why did Yahweh keep intruding into the affairs of his family? Couldn't God just let them alone to live their lives as they pleased?

Even sadder is verse 17: "So he died." But that verse does not fail to add that his death served one other purpose; it happened "according to the word of the LORD that Elijah had spoken." God was in charge. His word was king.

The Lord, who is always in charge, manifested Himself one more time in the recorded events of Elijah's life. That manifestation came in the spectacular way He removed His servant in 2 Kings 2:1-15. It is also seen in the repeated phrase that appears three times in verses 2,4 and 6, "the LORD has sent me."

It was on the eve of Elijah's translation that God prepared not only his servant Elijah, but Elisha, his understudy, and the other prophets who were studying to be ministers of the word. The ten years of internship for Elisha would now come to an end.

Elijah's last day on earth was a memorable day. As the two men walked along, revisiting many of the places where they had ministered the word together, their minds must have been filled with all the events of their ministry. It probably seemed like only yesterday that Elijah had thrown his mantle over Elisha's shoulders and the young farmer had responded so wonderfully.

As they walked, Elijah said repeatedly, "Stay here." It is not clear whether Elijah was testing Elisha's resolve, or if he was just a private person who wanted to be alone in this final moment before his departure. Some have speculated that this request was motivated by the prophet's modesty and humility. Regardless, Elijah did not guess that God had already revealed that his departure was at hand to all the sons of the prophets as well as to Elisha himself. By so doing, God had thereby set a miraculous seal on the life, work and especially the words of his servant Elijah.

ELISHA'S REQUEST

It was the Lord who impelled him to go on this one final journey to visit all the sites where these students were. Interestingly enough, God had led these men to set up schools for the prophets in the very citadels of pagan religion.

There was one at Bethel; that was the town where a bull was set up to represent the new religion of the realm — quite a symbol for a false religion! Just a lot of talk! But no power! Another was at Jericho; another at Gilgal, the city near the Jordan. Samuel had earlier established a school at Ramah (1 Samuel 19:18,23; 20:1).

But now Elijah wanted to visit the three schools he had founded, perhaps in order to strengthen and fortify the lives of his disciples and to consecrate them for their future ministry. The conclusion of the work he had begun, and for which he had despaired so grievously when he went so despondently to Mount Sinai, now rested with these men in the schools of the sons of the prophets and with Elisha.

Elijah was ready to make his last will and testament to Elisha. Ask what you wish, he said, before I am taken. Elisha's request was for a double portion of Elijah's spirit (verse 9). What Elisha desired more than anything else was not riches, greatness, fame, power, or to be remembered. In this case he "coveted earnestly the best gifts." Elisha's request was based on Deuteronomy 21:17, where the "double portion" represented the first-born's share of the inheritance. He did not mean to imply by this request for a double portion that he wanted to do twice the miracles of Elijah, nor that he would have twice the amount of the Holy Spirit's help that Elijah had had. Neither did he wish to have an evangelical, gracious spirit as opposed to Elijah's more so-called legal spirit.

Elisha asked that, in light of the great needs of the day, he might be granted a work of the Holy Spirit in his life similar to the work Elijah had received. But this request, as Elijah noted, was not Elijah's to give; that was the prerogative of the Holy Spirit. This was a difficult thing, yet as God had observed centuries earlier in the improbable situation in which Abraham found himself, "Is anything, then, too difficult for the LORD?" (Genesis 18:14).

However, if Elisha were to witness the translation of Elijah to heaven, his request would be granted. Presumably the sight of Elijah's ascension would strengthen and make more vivid Elisha's faith in the unseen world. That in turn would help him to depend more on the presence and power of God. He would inherit not only the usual share of the inheritance that all the sons usually got, but he would also receive as if it were the executor's portion as well — hence the double portion which usually went to the eldest son who also was the executor of the will.

A CHARIOT OF FIRE

Suddenly a chariot of fire and horses of fire separated them, and Elijah went up in a whirlwind. Such storms and sirocco-like winds normally were the heralds of theophanies (cf. Job 38:1; 40:6; Ezekiel 1:4; Zechariah 9:14). And so it was on that day as well.

God's servant died as he had lived — in the service of his Lord. Only death ended his rich and varied ministry for the Lord. When he left, so great was the vacuum and hole in Israel that Elisha could only exclaim, "My father, My father! The chariots and horsemen of Israel" (verse 12). What he meant was that his spiritual father who had nourished him in the word was now departing. But there was more. As Harry Blunt has written:

> Elisha, therefore, knew what alas few Christians ever dream of knowing, that the devout and holy followers of God, are the support and safeguard of their country . . . The real strength of our beloved country exists not in her fleets, her armies, her wealth, or even her free and invaluable institutions, and the high endowments of her senators, but simply and entirely in the blessings of her God and this will rest upon her in proportion as her governors are holy and God-fearing men and her inhabitants a religiously-instructed and a praying people. These are the chariots of Israel and the horsemen thereof. [1]

The removal of Elijah meant more than the removal of all of Israel's army. Her number one line of defense was exactly what the best line of defense is for any contemporary nation: When the righteous are removed, the loss is irreparable.

God must be in charge or all real controls are lost. He knows even the day of our death. He controls all things. Must we be warned once again, "Is it because there is no God in the land" that we act the way we do? It is high time for review of what God has done for us in the past, both individually and as larger units of families, churches, institutions, and nations. It is time we heed the accumulated markers He has left in our times and history. Righteous living and teaching are the hallmarks of a happy and free people. There, more than in all the missile silos of any modern power, lies the real hope for the future.

THE CHARIOT OF FIRE

2 Kings 1:6 — 2:13

1. In your opinion, why did God consume the first two squadrons of soldiers and spare the third? What might this tell us about the justice and mercy of God today?
2. If you were given the opportunity, like Elisha, to "ask what you wish" of God to help you be a stronger bearer of His Word, what one thing would you ask for? Why? What Scriptures can you think of that would indicate that God *wants* to meet your request?

10

The Secret of Elijah's Power
Matthew 17:1-13

More than any other person in the history of biblical revelation, Elijah demonstrated what can be expected of those who are filled with the Holy Spirit and power of God. Such longings are not irrelevant or unspiritual, for this man's life has been used in Scripture as a model to encourage us to expect some of the same types of magnificent feats of prayer, power, and evidences of the work of our Lord in His church.

In this sense, Elijah was only a harbinger, an earnest, or a downpayment on what was yet to be realized by believers before that great and terrible day of the Lord would come and the work of the church would come to an end. In fact, that is where we can begin. The last prophet of the Old Testament still recalled the brilliance of this man's life and what God had done through him. Predicted Malachi, "Behold, I will send you Elijah the prophet before the great and dreadful day of the LORD comes" (Malachi 4:5).

The reference, of course, was to none other than John the

103

Baptist — at least in its first or primary reference in history. If Elijah was the prototype, then John the Baptist certainly was in his line. But that is only the beginning statement, for Luke 1:17 makes it clear that John the Baptist did not finally fulfill this prophecy in any literal sense. Elijah himself, apparently, would return back to earth just before Christ returned in judgment at His second coming — perhaps as one of the two witnesses mentioned by the apostle John in Revelation 11. Luke's affirmation was that John the Baptist had come as Elijah in the sense that he came "in the spirit and the power of Elijah."

It is this clue which allows us to see Elijah in a whole new orientation. It is one that spells out a modeling role for this prophet that indeed has enormous implications for the church at large. If that same power which Elijah the prophet evidenced in his personal prayer life and on Mount Carmel could somehow be captured today, we indeed would see the power of God at work in ways reminiscent of Elijah's day. That is exactly what the text suggests about John the Baptist when it informs us that John came "in the spirit and the power of Elijah" (Luke 1:17).

"BUT WHAT ABOUT ME?"

Thus far we have not given much hope to the rather average person who sits in the pew and says, "But I'm neither Elijah nor John the Baptist. I'm just little old me — not a prophet or one of those special people in biblical times." But that is where our logic runs into a major mistake; for while we are not Elijah or John the Baptist in any literal sense, Scripture does make a direct association between ourselves and these men.

To begin where the New Testament picks this argument up, it is necessary to recall that there was a general expectation in those days that Elijah would come back and precede the arrival of the Messiah. That is why Jesus's disciples asked Him, "Why do the scribes say that first Elijah must come?" (Matthew 17:10).

Our Lord's answer at first sounds a bit like "double-talk," for He replied, "Elijah is coming [present tense] and he is to restore all things; but I tell you that Elijah has already come and they did to him whatever they pleased . . . Then the disciples understood that he was speaking about John the

Baptist" (Matthew 17:11-13; *cf.* Mark 9:13).

To complicate things a bit more for the moment, when John the Baptist was asked straight out if he was Elijah, he countered, "I am not."

They asked, "Are you a prophet?"

Again he answered, "No."

"Who are you then?" they badgered.

"I am a voice crying in the wilderness: 'Prepare the way of the LORD' " (John 1:21).

Do not conclude that the text cannot make up its mind or that there is a contradiction here. Jesus added on another occasion, "For all the law and the prophets prophesied until John; and if you are willing to accept it, he is Elijah who is to come" (Matthew 11:13,14). It is clear, then, that Jesus regarded John both in the sense of already fulfilling the prediction that Elijah was to come and yet as falling short of the total fulfillment which could only be realized in the future. Again, it becomes all the more important that we hear the angel's pledge at the announcement of the birth of John the Baptist. John would go before the Lord "in the spirit and the power of Elijah" (Luke 1:17). That is the statement which makes it possible for us to understand how Elijah could have come already in John the Baptist and how John absolutely could *not* have fulfilled everything the prophet Malachi had had in mind. There would be a coming of Elijah in the future just before the awful judgment of the last days connected with the second advent of Jesus Christ. (The reader who seeks a more technical discussion of this important distinction may read a fuller treatment of this matter in my book, *The Uses of the Old Testament in the New,* chapter 4, Chicago: Moody Press, 1985, pp. 77-88.)

JOHN HAD THE SAME POWER

The point we believe the Scripture establishes is that John had available the same spirit and the same power that Elijah had available for the tasks he performed in the Old Testament. But here then is the surprise: Jesus taught that "Among those born of women there has not arisen anyone greater than John the Baptist; yet he who is least in the kingdom of heaven is greater than he" (Matthew 11:11).

How could any of us in this New Testament era be greater

than John the Baptist, who came in the spirit and power of
the awesome Elijah? But we can, for that is what Jesus taught.
We too can pray, teach, minister, serve, give, help, and work
in a way so dynamic that it can be reminiscent only of the
magnificent deeds God accomplished through his servant Elijah.

No wonder James warns us not to make a special person
out of Elijah (James 5:17). Elijah was an ordinary man just
like ourselves, but when he prayed earnestly, it did not rain
for three and a half years. When he prayed again, it started
to rain! What a challenge for mighty, effective, and Spirit-filled
praying! James had just observed in the preceding verse (James
5:16) that the prayer that is energized (literally in the Greek,
that is "worked in") by the Holy Spirit and laid on the heart
of a righteous man is indeed powerful and effective.

THE TWO ELEMENTS OF ELIJAH'S POWER

No doubt, this is where the secret of Elijah's power began:
It began in prayer. But it had to also begin in the life of one
who had made a stand for righteousness and godly living. Our
Lord cannot use instruments that are stained by the world.
Give Him a clean vessel that has taken on the righteousness
of Christ and then add to that person a life of prayer in the
Spirit of God, and the world will soon see repeated what God
did for this prophet of old.

We cannot hold back anything. There must be no divided
or contrary purpose in our hearts other than to please our Lord.
For when we do meet these conditions, God will give to those
who obey His Holy Spirit. Acts 5:32 teaches, "We are witnesses
of these things and so is the Holy Spirit whom God has given
to those who obey him."

The Holy Spirit's dynamic and mighty work is not reserved
for a special class of worthies from another day; we too, like
John the Baptist and even exceeding him, can demonstrate the
same spirit and power of the God who worked in Elijah. The
Holy Spirit has already been given; there is no need to struggle,
writhe, agonize or enter into special pleading or vehement
entreaty. We must only be clean and desire to be filled with
the Holy Spirit.

In a similar manner, to exhibit the power of Elijah is to
do the same works that he did. Look at Elijah. He was generally
regarded as a rustic, unkempt, unpolished man from the hills

of Transjordania. He too had weaknesses, often in the very
places where we are weak. He too was tempted with similar
desires and passions as our own. He too knew what it meant
to fail and to fail royally in front of the wicked queen herself.
Yet that is not where he left the matter. Because God was
strong in him, he rose to check the rising tide of idolatry. He
found the strength and the purpose in life to go on in spite
of his natural timidity. He trained a successor who accomplished
every bit as much as he was able to do in his own lifetime.
He trained more future disciples, teachers, and prophets in the
colleges that he opened for teaching than any other Old Testament worthy.

Given this list of achievements, we are all the more
startled by the promise of our Lord that anyone who is least
in the kingdom of heaven is greater than John the Baptist — who
was both the fulfillment of the Elijah who was to come and
an earnest or downpayment on the final Elijah who would be
sent by God in the last days.

The countdown on God's finale to history has begun. But
at the center of the stage are those who obey Him and who
act in the spirit and power of Elijah. That is what is needed
at this hour more than anything else. So line up, you who
think you are nothing more than "little people." There is an
amazing job that is to be done and it ought to rival what
happened on Mount Carmel and the rest of the deeds of this
servant of God, Elijah.

John the Baptist is not the only insight we get into the
life of Elijah after he is gone. There is also that marvelous
encounter of the three disciples, who along with Jesus, experienced the unspeakably wonderful scene on the Mount of Trans-
figuration.

ELIJAH APPEARS WITH JESUS

It happened just a week after the famous incident at
Caesarea-Phillipi where Peter had made that great confession:
Jesus had asked who the disciples thought Jesus was, and Peter
had blurted out, "You are the Messiah, the Son of the living
God" (Matthew 16:16). Jesus praised Peter, but cautioned him
that what he had said was not from his own ingenuity; rather,
it was a revelation from his Father in heaven.

Then He took Peter, James and John up into a high

mountain by themselves. On this occasion our Lord would fortify Himself for the great spiritual and physical conflict that was to come in Jerusalem where the Son of Man would be hauled off to be crucified. But He would prepare for this coming conflict by entering into prayer.

As Jesus entered into the work of prayer, the disciples entered into sleep and were barely awake when suddenly Jesus was transfigured right before their eyes (Matthew 17:1-8; Mark 9:2-8; Luke 9:28-36). So radiant was the change that took place in Jesus as He was praying that "his face shone as the sun" (Matthew 17:2). The illumination, however, was no doubt from within rather than reflecting any outside luminary or glory. Thus, for a brief moment, the Shekinah glory itself broke out on the one who Himself was and is the glory of God. This was only a brief anticipation of that glory that was soon to be His on a permanent basis — a glory which He had had with the Father, but which He had voluntarily laid aside until He had finished the work His Father had sent Him to do.

Jesus's clothes became dazzling white, bright as a flash of lightning. This sight must have been resplendent against the dark blue sky. Here was another reminder of the appearances of Christ in the Old Testament in the pillar of fire, the cloud of glory by day, the burning bush, the thunders and lightnings of Sinai and on numerous occasions when the Lord fought for Israel.

Suddenly, two men appeared with Jesus: Moses and Elijah. "But why these two?" we ask. No doubt to affirm the glory, dignity, and triumphant success of Christ before Jesus and His disciples faced the darkest hour they had ever entered. To counterbalance the shame, ignominy, and disgrace of this hour, the blazing glory of God anticipated the triumphant conclusion to what, for the moment, would look like disaster and total defeat.

Moses, the founder of the law, who had power to turn the waters into blood and to smite the earth with every plague, and Elijah, who had power to shut up the heavens so that it did not rain, both appeared in conversation with their Lord on the mountain.

WHAT MOSES, ELIJAH AND JESUS TALKED ABOUT

What on earth could have been the topic of conversation

between these three? The theme of their conversation was nothing less than the "exodus" or "departure" that He was subsequently to accomplish at Jerusalem (Luke 9:31). This is hardly a surprise, for their own salvation, just as much as ours, depended on the outcome of what took place on the cross in Jerusalem. Their only hope lay where ours does — not in the merits of their deeds, but in the work of Christ on their behalf.

Moses and Elijah were not singled out because they were such super saints; Moses' petulance and Elijah's fretfulness and cowardice were already in the book. But the great themes of both of these men as recipients of revelation might easily have been the object of some most wonderful conversation as it related to the theme of redemption.

Moses might well have dwelt on how Jesus must die as the lamb of God, the goat of the Day of Atonement. The great themes that our Lord had given to him in the Levitical instructions were now to have their one and only final fulfillment. The blood of bulls and goats could never take away sin (Hebrews 10:1,2); however, neither did the Old Testament ever claim or teach that such blood could or did take away sins. Instead, it argued that forgiveness was indeed available on the grounds that God said it was available; the sin offerings which accompanied that forgiveness were merely pictures of that special work which was yet to come. And here now was the moment which everyone had anticipated as Moses, Elijah and Christ discussed Jesus' "departure" which was to take place shortly in Jerusalem. What a fantastic discussion this must have been!

No less exciting must have been the contribution of the prophet Elijah. Surely he must have interjected a word about the glory that should now belong to the Father when He accomplished all that He had planned from eternity. The same glory which boldly thundered down on Mount Carmel and which Elijah had caught a glimpse of from his despondent location in the cave on Mt. Sinai would now break forth on Easter Sunday morning and radiate all over the world.

Both these subjects, of course, were well known by our Lord. It was He who had first given them to the same two men who now conversed with Him. Yet, the very thought of these topics must have strengthened and gladdened our Lord's heart as He faced now the darkest moment that heaven has ever, or ever will, face.

So went the conversation between two mortals who had left this world under most unusual circumstances. Moses had died not of natural causes, but under the tender and special circumstances prepared by God. Elijah had not gone through the experience of death, but like Enoch, he had been ushered into glory and the presence of God without going through the act of dying. In fact, Elijah was transported in a whirlwind in the twinkling of an eye from earth into the presence of our Lord. Some deal, right?

THE FOCAL POINT

Thus the one of whom Moses in the law and Elijah in the prophets wrote was now on earth discussing what was to shortly take place — all of which had been anticipated in the writings of Scripture as represented by these two men (Jeremiah 1:45).

This, then, is where we come into the picture again. What Moses and Elijah here experience was only an earnest or a downpayment on what we too can and probably already have begun to experience. We can now begin to participate in the benefits of the death and resurrection of our Lord. For just as the theme of their conversation was our Lord's "departure," so we too ought to concentrate on this aspect of our Lord's work more than any other. Moses and Elijah did not focus on Jesus's philanthropy, the insight of His teachings, His identification with the poor, His demand for social justice, or even the mystery of His incarnation. All of these legitimate topics were dwarfed by the magnitude of His death and its effects upon us.

The New Testament maintains this same fine tradition and emphasis. There are some 175 passages in the New Testament which focus on Christ's death. Surely no fair exegete can afford to miss the significance of this fact.

Accordingly, the closer we get to the cross in our theology, and the more we meditate on that event and what it accomplished for each of us, the closer we will come to the heart and the center of our faith. To realize the implications of being witnesses to the removal of our sin and to seeing the impact that the glory of God can have on us, our culture and day, is breathtaking indeed. This truly was God's Son, whom the Father had chosen;

we ought to listen to Him (Luke 9:35).

THE SECRET OF ELIJAH'S POWER

Matthew 17:1-13

1. If Acts 5:32 promises the Holy Spirit to all who obey God, what does this mean to you, today? In what "impossible" tasks could the power of the Holy Spirit who indwelt Elijah be evidenced today if we obey? What do you think impedes the effectiveness of many believers today?
2. What were the two elements of the secret of Elijah's power? On a scale of 1 to 10, rate your personal effectiveness in these two aspects. Prayerfully think through some lifestyle strategies that will help you become more like Elijah in these areas.
3. God's Spirit turned one ordinary man into a catalyst for positive change. Jesus said we would have the same power to do similar and even greater works. What types of changes in society do you sense God is placing on your heart to bring about? With the Holy Spirit guiding and empowering you, is there any reason such changes could never happen?

11

What's Left To Do for a Finale?
Revelation 11:3-19

There is one more important episode in our study on Elijah. This one is found in Revelation 11:3-19. It is the disclosure of the future appearance of the two brave witnesses who will minister in the holy city of Jerusalem just before the Lord returns.

Now some Christians get nervous when the subject turns to the book of Revelation. This is unnecessary, since the book is primarily a book of worship and it is "the revelation of Jesus Christ" (Revelation 1:1). What could be a greater topic of interest than that? In fact, the scene that dominates the whole book is the depiction of the throne of God about which are gathered all who have entered into glory and are now praising the Lamb for His work in creation and redemption (Revelation 4-5).

But the two witnesses mentioned in the eleventh chapter of Revelation are of special interest to us, for one of those witnesses just may well be our Tishbite Elijah. Remember how

Malachi promised that Elijah would come back just before the great and dreadful day of the Lord (Malachi 4:5)? Also, that Jesus said John the Baptist had only fulfilled the spirit and the power of Elijah (Luke 1:17), but that Elijah still must come prior to the second coming even as the scribes had taught in Jesus' day? This then could well be the additional revelation that we need to complete the picture.

TWO MEN PREACH REPENTANCE: MOSES AND ELIJAH?

The text of Revelation predicts that two men will stand up and preach repentance for 1,260 days (approximately three and a half years) in Jerusalem. These two are the same two olive trees the prophet Zechariah had anticipated in his predictions (Zechariah 4). Thus, much as Joshua the High Priest and Zerubbabel the governor of Judah stood before the Lord to serve in the post-exilic days of the prophet Zechariah, so these two witnesses will stand before God to serve Him just before the great climax to history.

The emphasis of Zechariah 4:3 is still where it was in the life of Elijah and in the life of John the Baptist, however. The prophet Zechariah announced, "Not by might, nor by power, but by my Spirit, says the LORD of hosts." And that is where the issue still rests for us as well. It is still a matter of the infilling of the Holy Spirit and the power of God for the mission of the church which God has given to us, just as it was for John in Luke 1:17 and even for Elijah's successor, Elisha, who prayed for a double portion of Elijah's spirit (2 Kings 2:9).

The fact that these two witnesses in Revelation 11 could be Moses and Elijah back on earth once again is suggested by the powers that they exhibit: "These men have power to shut up the sky so that it will not rain during the time they are prophesying [that sounds like Elijah]; and they have power to turn water into blood and to strike the earth with every kind of plague as often as they wish [that sounds like Moses]" (Revelation 11:6).

"THE BEAST" MAKES HIS ENTRANCE

However, they are not left unopposed. Suddenly "the beast" is introduced in verse 7. This character seems to be none other than the same one who is called "the man of lawlessness" in 2 Thessalonians 2:3, or the "little horn" in Daniel 7:21. This monster will oppose the preaching of these two preachers of the gospel. Moreover, he will kill both of them and leave their bodies to rot in the streets of Jerusalem, where our Lord had been crucified (verses 7,8). So relieved will be the men and women of every language, tribe and nation that these two prophets of doom and coming judgment are gone, that they will all send gifts to one another as if it were Christmas (verses 9,10).

The bodies of the two men will lay for three and a half days while all this wild rejoicing goes on that the preachers have been silenced and society's conscience can now be free — or so they will think. For three and a half days men and women, children and animals will gawk and gaze on the fallen bodies of these men of great power and conviction.

Suddenly, in the midst of all the partying and giving of gifts, God will grant to his two witnesses life and vitality once again. Can you imagine what consternation that will cause?

This in turn will be followed with the blast of a loud voice that will blare out, "Come up here," and they will once again disappear from the view of mortals as they ascend up to heaven in a cloud (verse 12).

THEN THE FUN BEGINS

Then the real fun will begin — fun at least for all those who have ever tasted the bitter dregs of unfairness and injustice and prayed, "How long, Lord Jesus, will all this suffering continue to go on? And You do not seem to do anything about it at all." For in that very same hour there will be such a giant earthquake that a tenth part of the city of Jerusalem will collapse (verse 13) and 7000 people will be killed. The survivors will be stupefied with terror and will give glory to the God of heaven. Then will it come to pass — earth's finest hour. "The kingdom of this world [will have] become the kingdom of our Lord and of his Christ, and he will reign for ever and ever" (verse 15).

Then it will be that God will have taken His power and His rightful authority and begun His reign over all the earth and over all creatures (verse 17). With that the temple in heaven will have been opened and there will be seen the Ark of the

Covenant (verse 19). What a spectacular display of the power, might, authority and dominion of our Lord.

Then it will also be that we shall rule and reign with Christ forever and forever. Eternity will only have begun.

Is it any wonder, then, that as believers we find all that is so central and dear to us in this prophet Elijah? He who was so filled with the spirit and power of the Lord; he who saw so vividly the glory of God as God caused all His goodness to pass by him in front of that cave on Mt. Sinai; he who had so remarkable a conversation which anticipated all that our Lord would accomplish at Calvary; and he who likewise will be filled with remarkable power and great joy as he anticipates the momentary second return of our Lord and His eternal rule over everything.

Truly Elijah was and still will be a forerunner of our Lord and His glory. But he also is by the same token an earnest of all of us who now come in his train and thereby experience the same remarkable power that he did. James was more than justified in holding him up as a model of effective prayer. The gospel writers were also correct in suggesting that others such as ourselves could experience and employ the same spirit and power of Elijah. And John, in the book of Revelation, was likewise suggestive in helping us to orient our thinking, living, praying and serving properly when he warned us how fantastically sensational and total will be the triumph of our Lord Jesus Christ shortly after these two witnesses conclude their final days of ministry here on earth.

What greater motivational information could we ask for? What more would we need to know or have by way of equipping power in order to carry out the task of evangelism, missions, discipleship, and effective prayer in the church of Christ? It is difficult to conceive of anything else. The finale of earth's history will be greater than all the hype of all the Superbowl football games and all of the most awesome inaugural ceremonies we have ever seen on planet Earth. No wonder Paul concludes a similar discussion of the great work of God in the resurrection of those who have died in Christ by urging, "Therefore brethren, be steadfast, unmovable and always abounding in the work of the Lord since you know that your labors are not in vain" (1 Corinthians 15:58). Only then will we too be harbingers, earnests, downpayments on Messiah's present work and on His soon return with great glory.

WHAT'S LEFT TO DO FOR A FINALE?

Revelation 11:3-19

1. As you read about the grand finale of earth as we know it and the beginnings of eternity, what emotions or thoughts did you experience? What do you imagine it will be like to rule and reign with Christ?
2. From your study of Elijah, list at least three character traits of the prophet that you would like to emulate in your personal walk with God and in your ministry to others.
3. Read 1 Corinthians 15:58 aloud. In what specific ways would you like to be "always abounding in the work of the Lord" in the coming months? (List several.) What is your motivation for doing so?

Appendix A
Diagrams of the Elijah Context

A. 1 and 2 Kings: Historical Divisions

		Divided Kingdom 28 Chapters				
	United Monarchy			Judean Kingdom		
2 Chapters	9 Chapters	11 Chapters	17 Chapters	6 Chapters	2 Chapters	
1　　2	3　　11	12　　22	1　　17	18　　23	24　　25	

|◄————— 1 Kings —————►|◄————— 2 Kings —————►|

B. Theological Context
THE WORD OF GOD
(over 100 references in 1 and 2 Kings)

Climactic
Center
of
1 and 2 Kings:
1 Kings 19:15-18

THE WORD OF GOD
CONCERNING:

19:15	19:16a	19:16b	19:17	19:18
1 Kings 20	1 Kings 21,22	2 Kings 1,2	2 Kings 3-17	2 Kings 18-25
A Change in the King of SYRIA	A Change in the King of ISRAEL	A Change in the Prophet to ISRAEL: ELISHA	The Swords of Syria, Israel, and the Prophet	A Remnant in spite of the Destruction of Jerusalem

C. Sections of 1 and 2 Kings

Solomon's Reign	58 Years of the Divided Kingdom	Ministry of Elijah	Ministry of Elisha	Fall of Israel	Fall of Judah
1 Kings 1-11	1 Kings 12-16	1 Kings 17- 2 Kings 2:13	2 Kings 2:14 — 13:21	2 Kings 13:22 — 17:41	2 Kings 18-25

Appendix B
For Further Study

Allen, Ron B., "Elijah The Broken Prophet," *Journal of Evangelical Theological Society* 22 (1979): 193-202.

Farrar, F.W., *First Book of Kings* Minneapolis: Klock and Klock, 1981 reprint.

Getz, Gene, *Power Under Pressure: Elijah* Chicago: Moody Press, 1983.

Hendricks, H.G., *Elijah: Confrontation, Conflict, and Crisis* Chicago: Moody 1972.

Keller, W. Phillip, *Elijah: Prophet of Power* Waco, Texas: Word Books, 1980.

Krummacher, F.W., *Elijah The Tishbite* American Tract Society, n.d.

MacDuff, John Ross, *Elijah, The Prophet of Fire* Grand Rapids: Baker, 1956.

Meyer, F.B., *Elijah: And The Secret of His Power* Fort Washington, Pennsylvania: Christian Literature Crusade, 1972.

Petersen, William J., *Meet Me on The Mountain* Wheaton, Illinois: Victor Books, 1979.

Pink, A.W., *The Life of Elijah* London: Banner of Truth Trust, 1963.

Rowley, H.H., "Elijah on Mount Carmel," in *Men of God* London: Nelson, 1963.

Van't Veer, M.B., *My God is Yahweh: Elijah and Ahab in an Age of Apostasy* tr. Theadore Plantraga, St. Catharines, Ontario: Paideia Press, 1980.

Wood, L.J., *Elijah The Prophet of God* Des Plaines, Illinois: Regular Baptist Press, 1968.

Notes

Chapter 1
1. Leviticus 11:15; 14:14.
2. M. B. Van't Veer, *My God Is Yahweh: Elijah and Ahab in an Age of Apostasy,* trans. Theodore Plantinga (St. Catharines, Ontario: Paideia Press, 1980), p. 73.

Chapter 3
1. A. W. Pink, *The Life of Elijah* (London, Banner of Truth, 1956), p. 109.
2. Josephus, *Antiquites* VIII, 13.2.

Chapter 4
1. A. W. Pink, *The Life of Elijah,* p. 127.

Chapter 5
1. C. F. Keil and Franz Delitzsch, *Biblical Commentary on the Old Testament: The Books of the Kings,* tr. James Martin, Grand Rapids: Eerdmans, 1950, p. 253.

Chapter 6
1. M. B. Van't Veer, *My God Is Yahweh,* pp. 391-93.

Chapter 7
1. A. W. Pink, *The Life of Elijah,* pp. 253-54.
2. Pink, p. 257.
3. Harold S. Kushner, *When Bad Things Happen to Good People,* New York: Schocken Books, 1981.

Chapter 8
1. A. W. Pink, *The Life of Elijah,* pp. 283-84.

Chapter 9
1. Henry Blunt, *Lectures on the History of Abraham, Jacob and Elisha,* (Philadelphia, Hooker, 1854), p. 217.